Cadbury's
Third Book of
Children's
Poetry

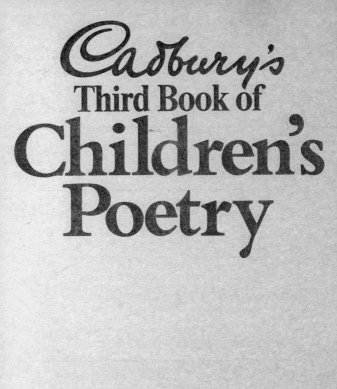

Beaver B

D0417971

A Beaver Book
Published by Arrow Books Limited
17–21 Conway Street, London W1P 6JD

An imprint of the Hutchinson Publishing Group

London Melbourne Sydney Auckland
Johannesburg and agencies throughout the world

First published 1985
© Cadbury Ltd 1985

Set in Linoterm Souvenir Light by
JH Graphics Limited, Reading

Printed and bound in Great Britain by
Cox & Wyman Limited, Reading

ISBN 0 09 944710 X

Contents

Publisher's note

The poems in this book were chosen by a panel of judges which included poets, teachers and educationalists, from nearly 20,000 entries for the Cadbury's National Exhibition of Children's Art 1985/6. This year is the third in which there has been a poetry section and the judges – Joan Freeman, educational psychologist; Jack Dalglish, Staff Inspector of English and poet; Vernon Scannell, poet; and Jennifer Curry, anthologist and author – were delighted at the great variety of material. They chose as outstanding the work of Rosemary Cowan and Emma Payne, whose poems appear on pages 52, 108, 168 and 176, and 80, 81, 101 and 107 respectively.

Rosemary Cowan, from Londonderry, is now eighteen years old and currently taking 'A' levels. She hopes to go on to read English or Media Studies at university. Rosemary has written poems and stories since she was very young and also enjoys playing tennis, travelling and photography.

Sixteen-year-old Emma Payne lives in London and is currently sitting her 'O' levels. She hopes to go on to university and eventually to take up a literary career. Emma's poems are based mainly on aspects of life in London and her work also appears in the *Cadbury's First and Second Books of Children's Poetry*. She enjoys fencing and playing the drums.

The judges also highly commended twenty children whose poems appear on pages, 12, 26, 27, 30, 32, 39, 44, 53, 58, 85, 90, 114, 125, 130, 133, 148, 151, 179, 186.

The poems have been arranged under subjects which gives the reader the opportunity to compare the ideas of children from as young as six to mature seventeen year olds. All the illustrations are taken from entries to the Art and Craft section of this year's Exhibition, and they complement the poems in an unusual and satisfying way.

We are very happy to be publishing such an interesting and original book and would like to thank all the writers and artists for their superb efforts. Don't forget, there's another chance to see your poem in print in the fourth *Cadbury's Book of Poetry* to be published in 1986. For details on how to enter next year's competition please turn to page 200.

Foreword

This year the poetry section attracted more than 30,000 entries and has gained an important place within Cadbury's National Exhibition of Children's Art.

Our thanks must go to the many teachers, educationalists and poets who have the difficult task of judging the entries, a task which becomes more challenging as the numbers increase and standards rise.

We sincerely hope that you will derive as much pleasure from reading the work of these young poets as we have done and that you will share our admiration for the talents of today's youth.

It is perhaps appropriate that less fortunate children should benefit from the efforts of those who have taken part in the competition. Cadbury Limited are therefore again donating a royalty from the sale of this book to the Save the Children Fund.

Adrian Cadbury

Cadbury's Third Book of Children's Poetry

AWARD WINNERS – Poetry Section
38th National Exhibition of Children's Art 1985/86

1985 ITALIAN TOUR AWARD
Emma Payne (16)
Hackney, London
Rosemary Cowan (17)
Portstewart, Co. Londonderry

SCHOOL POETRY AWARD
The King's School, Canterbury, Kent

HIGHLY COMMENDED
7 and under

Dheya Biswas (6) Bedgrove County First School, Aylesbury, Bucks
Kristy Derbyshire (7) St. John's C.E. Primary School, Dukinfield
Robin Lewis Gillyon (7) Bedgrove County First School, Aylesbury, Bucks
Rosie Hunter (6) Stroud, Glos
Tracy Linda Stevens (7) Tunbury County Primary School,
Walderslade, Kent

8–11

Debbie Church (9) St Patrick's School, Troon, Ayrshire
David C. S. Harman (10) The Beacon School, Amersham, Bucks
Susie Moore (11) Borth, Dyfed
Leoma Rushton (9) Bontddn, Dolgellau, Gwynedd

12–14

Katherine Goodwin (14) The Mountbatten School, Romsey, Hants
Lucas David Marshall (14) The Mountbatten School, Romsey, Hants
Sarah Jane Ratheram (14) Harborne, Birmingham
Adam Stanley (13) Alcombe, Minehead, Somerset
Emily Wilson (13) Sidcot School, Winscombe, Avon

15–17

Jon Harley (16) Barnard Castle, Co. Durham
Arnold Hunt (15) Hendon, London
James W. S. Loxley (16) Fiddlers Hamlet, Epping, Essex
Catherine Skinner (16) Hitchin, Herts

I, Myself

Just a Thought

I, myself. Myself, I.
I, myself can only see another.
I, myself cannot see me as myself.
I can see myself as a reflection, although I cannot see
myself like I see you.

You, yourself. Yourself you.
You yourself can only see another.
You yourself cannot see yourself.
You can see yourself as a reflection, although,
you cannot see yourself like you see me.

Anita Seehra (17) Belvedere, Kent

A Siesta

The little black ant,
Determined as ever,
Crawls over my finger.
As he reaches the top,
He turns and looks up at me,
Smiling wisely to himself.

Mummy is stretched out
On the grey prickly rug,
Her hat pulled over her eyes.
Her hair is entwined
With the blades of grass,
Glistening in the sun.

There's a daisy right in front of my nose,
With a drop of dew on one petal.
A sparkling spider's web
Is stranded from it,
To a nearby companion.

Sheba bounds over to me,
Her eyes bright and evil.
Her black fur is warm and soft
As she pounces on my leg.
She sits down
On the edge of the rug
And carefully preens a whisker.
Her deep purr sounds.

I can hear a bird
Twittering furiously
In an overhead tree.
It swoops down into sight.
Sheba watches the little bird's antics
With a half-opened eye.

My back is getting sticky,
My bonnet's irritating me.
I let out a cry,
Startling Sheba, waking Mummy.
She slowly stirs.
'Shush, darling,
Time to go in.'
Her voice coos softly.

I'm hoisted over a hip,
And I bury my face
In her soft pullover.
It tastes nice.
I watch her hair swing,
Back and forth,
Back and forth.
My eyes close,
And the world drifts out.

Emily Wilson (13)
Sidcot School, Winscombe, Avon
(Highly commended)

The Early Days

LIFE'S DAWN
Day 1
The first light is vague.
I'm screaming, others are screaming.
I'm feeble, helpless,
Groping about in the darkness,
Longing for the cock crow.

MID-MORNING
Day 4836
Time for a break, nearing lunch.
A little empty hole in my mind,
Waiting to be filled with knowledge.
It is a long time since the dawn,
But the night is still far away.

Fiona O'Neill (13)
Cookstown, Co. Tyrone, N. Ireland

I Have Been Here Before

I have been here before,
Have I been trapped in time?
Have I gone back like an old record stuck in its
    groove?
I remember my puppy rushing ahead along the path,
William and Phillip running in the dips,
A train going under the bridge stirring cows.
What is happening?
I have been here before.

James Walsh (10) The Beacon School, Amersham, Bucks

'Field Patterns', Alex Brooks (17)

I Am Your Child

Even as I was drawn from my protected world,
And I breathed the first air into my lungs,
Even as the dried blood was washed from my
    screaming face,
And I was placed into the arms of an enveloping
    blanket,
I was secure.

Even through the years of dawning awareness,
And frustrated mumblings used as a cover of protest,
Even through knocked knees and bloody bruises,
And arguments over religion and politics,
I was safe.
            For I am your child,
Seventeen, mature, reliable, sensible.
A child with ordinary looks – but extraordinary
    parents.
A child who is not a child – but is close.
A child who is an individual – but looks like everyone
    else.

Read my mind,
And count the cells siphoned from
My Mother
and
My Father.
Read their talents in my fingertips
And smell their emotions spinning around my soul.
I am your child,
So different
Yet so alike.

Denise Wright (17) Walsall, West Midlands

I Love

I love my techer
Cos I love my worc
and I love my sista
beter than my tedi bers.

Sue Arrowsmith (4)
Strathalmond Park,
Edinburgh

My Teeth

I am losing my teeth
I have lost two
If I lose any more
I won't be able to chew.

Jennifer Godfrey (5)
Crofty, Swansea,
W. Glamorgan

'A Visit to the Dentist'. Steven Peall and Robert Page (7)

17

Temptations

I wish I could –
    Smash my sister's toys up
    Squirt my mum's washing on the line,
    Rip pages out of a book,
    Cut somebody's hair until they're bald,
    Tip paint all over the floor!

Griffith Hewis (6)
Richmond Primary School, Hinckley, Leics

Myself

There, in the photo, in a life of my own,
I sit, a shoe missing, on a rush mat.
Oblivious of my whereabouts, I gaze
At the little white men waiting,
Then running, and waiting again.

'Well run!' shouts Daddy and I
Smack the ground in delight.
I wonder why I sit here,
Carrying out minor repairs on my toy car,
In a cricket net.

I glare at the camera with my
Chubby face. I smile and even
Manage to look photogenic.
I sit, all two and a half feet of me,
With a lead round my chest.

Now my life no longer belongs to me;
I am never caught with shoes missing.
I still gaze at the little white men,
With more interest than before;
I watch them run and stop. And run.

I am no longer so excited when
My father shouts. He is no longer
The captain, but an umpire, I fear.
I no longer repair toy cars of the '60s,
But wait and fiddle with cars of the '80s.

I am no longer so photogenic –
Indeed I am usually the other side of the lens.
I work and wait, all five feet nine of me,
For the day I take exams, and I still
Struggle to get the lead off me.

Jeremy Barnes (14) St Catherine's,
Guildford, Surrey

I Hate Playtimes

I hate school, I hate school,
I hate the playtimes
I don't have anybody to play with
and most of them are running around
and playing games
and I don't have anybody to play with
and sometimes I just lie on the log
and sometimes I just stand in a shelter.

Matthew Whalley (6)
Simpson County Combined School,
Milton Keynes

Dear Sir

Dear Sir, I'm sorry about my misbehaviour,
So that's why I'm writing this letter,
I'm sorry about your broken leg,
I hope it's getting better.

I'm sorry about the poison ivy,
I'm sorry about the snake,
I'm sorry I didn't realize,
That your life was at stake.

I'm sorry about the itching powder,
That I put down your back,
I honestly didn't mean,
To get you the sack.

I'm sorry about the curry powder,
That I put in your tea,
I'm sorry about the pin on your seat,
I'm glad you didn't see me.

I'm sorry I made you break your table,
I know you went crazy when you got the bill,
I actually didn't mean . . . (I'm sorry),
To make you very ill.

I'm sorry about the bar of soap,
That I set outside the door,
The jokes have gone a little too far,
I promise there won't be any more.

So ends this letter of apology,
I hope you will accept,
I always thought you were a clever guy,
Who would have looked before you leapt!

Stephen Dow (11)
St Anne's Primary School, Finaghy, Belfast

Photographs

I have only been in the paper once,
At my first school,
The photograph was long,
Long and thin,
I was second from the end.
I stood there smiling
Waiting for the trigger to click
My friend was next to me,
Waiting too.
Then it clicked
And the photograph was taken.
Next day, there we were
In the paper.
A humble little school,
In the long, thin photograph.
With me there,
Next to my friend,
In the only picture in the paper,
In my life.

Nicholas Grant (10)
High Wycombe, Bucks

Sometimes I Wake

Sometimes I wake up so frightened
I feel as if a black pit had appeared
Beneath my feet. I totter on the
Edge, afraid of untold depths and sheer sides.
I long to curl up animal-like and
Escape the dull beat of the doom-laden drum.

Yet society cannot understand and so will not permit it.
I must put on a cheerful, care-free face.
I hide my terror beneath a thin facade and
Hope that no one looks too closely,
Asks too many questions and
Sees the cracks through which helplessness leaks.

It would be nice to give in.
Let the darkness swamp me and drink its
Poison. Feel its coldness wash over my head,
But I cannot allow myself such luxury.
To struggle no more is to die.
Let it be better to wake up screaming.

Joanna Brown (15) Winterton, S. Humberside

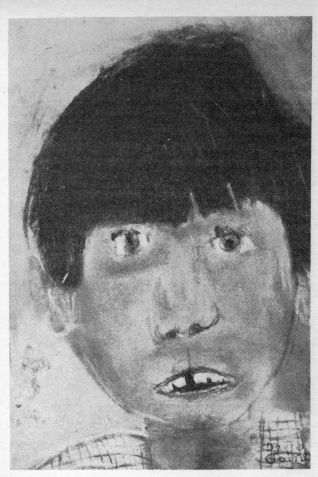

'This is Me'. David Johnson (7) (Highly commended)

My Fight

It all started by my friend
pinching me.
I pinched him back,
and then we started to fight.
We started kicking and punching,
Biff Baff ooooh,
ooo that hurt, kick.
I put my fist up
I punched him.
Everybody shouts and screams,
Everybody is joining in.
Everybody is kicking and thumping,
they all shout ooooh ooo.
Then my Mummy comes outside,
She sees it and stops it.
So we have to stop it and make friends again.

Jamie Vacca (7)
Thorpe Junior School, Peterborough, Cambs

War of Words

A pressurized build up,
Steaming inside me,
Bursts out through my mouth
In a broken torrent of insults.
Argument. Hate.
It is my turn now,
I have endured the insults,
I have borne the hate,
And kept my temper.
Why should I tolerate him?
Madness flares within my bitter mind.
Fuelled by a frowning dark hate,
I release the heat from weeks of friction;
Anger, aggression and irritation
Flow from my mouth like hot acid.

My storm subsides,
Leaving a heavy silence.
We stare at each other,
Trying to burn the other with our eyes.
I turn, and walk slowly away,
Feeling no regret.
Hate.

Timothy Smith (14)
The King's School, Canterbury, Kent

I'm Alright

Don't bother me,
I'm alright.
Take your troubles elsewhere.
Don't spoil my life,
With your problems.
I'm not interested: I don't care.

Go and bother someone else;
Tell them your worries and fears.
Go to someone who'll listen;
And won't block their ears.
Who'll pay some attention,
And help put you right.
But don't bother me:
I'm alright.

Sally Parker (13) Lymm, Cheshire

Someone

Will someone let the cat in.
Will someone make the tea.
Will someone tidy their bedroom.
Oh why is that someone Me?

Will someone lay the table.
Will someone comb their hair.
Will someone please stop talking.
Oh It Just isn't Fair.

Rosie Hunter (6) Stroud, Glos
(Highly commended)

A Visit to the Doctor

I went to the doctor's
And guess what I had!

I had spots on my bots,
And splinters in my knickers,
And I hid in the loo
Because I had flu,
And tonsillitis
And fleabiters.
I was down in the dumps
Because I had mumps
And bumps
And lumps,
And even my toy beaver
Had a dose of the fever.

The doctor said, 'Try these!
Here's pink pills and green pills and blue pills
And horrible medicine.'
Ugh!

Robin Gillyon (7)
Bedgrove County First School,
Aylesbury, Bucks
(Highly commended)

High Dive

The little trot on the blue, gridded rubber,
The slight spring and bending of fear-struck frail
    knees,
The churning of the stomach, the tense neatness,
As I follow my fear over the edge into an
    unsupporting silence.
With my feet above me I gaze down one hundred feet
Towards an awaiting, tiny rectangle of soft, bubbling
    water,
That split second of stillness, hours.
I see everything below.
Thousands of people, jarring necks, flicking cameras.
As the diving board of safety just an immense metre
    away.
Then down, spins, twirls, naturally somersaulting,
    half twisting and piking,
Flying like a swallow soaring towards its prey,
Every turn, every spin,
Eyeing the distance to the water.
Accelerating as a sky-diver, but neatly as a high-diver,
The plain spot of deflecting foam grows,
Harder, larger, ready to swallow me, a struggling
    prey.
Falling.
Faster.
Faster.
Towards the awaiting mouth of spitting white.
Then into a fixed swallow position.
Plummeting down into a straight, tense and prepared
    dive.

Like an arrow, my hands ahead, I pierce the water,
Slowly, surely curving back up to the surface
For a long awaited breath.
Relaxation.
Out, now, of freedom and danger.
Back into a seizing gravity of motherly protection and
   safety.

Christopher Calthrop (13)
The King's School, Canterbury, Kent

1984

I'm unapproved, unbeknown
Uncared for, uncredited
Undecided, uneducated
Unequal, unessential
Unfamed, unfashionable
Unfortunate, unfunded
Unhappy, unhoused
Unimportant, unloved
Unknowable, unmerited
Unnoticed, unpractical
Unrefined, unremembered
Unsatisfactory, unsheltered
Unsophisticated, untaught
Untrained, unversed
UNEMPLOYED!!

Alison Fell (14) Filey, N. Yorks

The Colour of My Eyes

A year ago, before the darkness came,
Spring arrived early.
The leaves were so green
And the stream so full after the rain
That now, as I feel warm sun on my face,
And hear the skylark high above,
It could have been just yesterday.
I remember quite clearly the summer that followed;
Long days of shimmering heat
That made August dry and dusty.
Corn ripened quickly and by September,
The bramble and elder
Were weighted down with their fruit.
Still I remember the blue of the sky
And the blue of the sea,
Both the colour of my eyes.
That was a year ago;
Sometimes yesterday,
Sometimes a lifetime away.
The memory will fade, as the light did
Before the voice came to tell me why,
Before the night came without a moon
Or the promise of dawn.
'There is no known cure . . .'
What if I'd known that before?

Katherine Goodwin (14) Romsey, Hants
(Highly commended)

My Reflection

That face in the mirror,
I see every day,
Copies all that I do,
And all that I say.
I can't catch it out,
It's staring at me,
But sometimes I wonder
If it sees what I see?
If I try and be quick
And leave it behind,
It quickens up with me,
It must read my mind!
I wish it would go, and leave me in peace,
When will your mimicking ever cease?
Which is real, me or you?
You look identical to me, too!
I'd like to push you away, then you'd be gone
But when I leave the room,
Do you live on?

Katherine Lloyd (10)
Padgate C.E. School, Warrington

'Portrait', Kim Foungli (12)

A Prophecy (of old age)

At 40 I'll stop work.
I'll sculpt, paint and grow a beard.
I'll write poetry under a pseudonym.

At 50 I'll pretend to have lost
all the taste I ever had.
I'll wear contrasting, checked trousers
and maroon ties.

At Christmas I'll give ugly, useless,
but expensive presents.
I'll frequent book shops
just for the music.

At 60 I'll change from checked, to pale grey
and accept old age.
I'll grow plump and let my beard
go grey.

When at last I'm 70,
I'll retire to the greenhouse
and propagate geraniums.
I'll burn incense, read the Koran
and send risqué postcards
to The Dali Lahma,
TIBET.
I'll have my wheel-chair
face towards Mecca
and experiment with yoga.

If at 80 I'm still animate,
I'll swim in the frozen Thames,
and cross the Pacific
in a bath-tub.
I'll bake mince pies
and entertain carol singers.

However, at 90
I'm sure to be pushing up . . .
. . . DUMBELLS.

Adam Stanley (13)
Alcombe, Minehead, Somerset
(Highly commended)

Skating

When I try to skate
My feet are so wary
They grit and grate;
And then I watch Mary
Easily gliding
Like an ice-fairy;
Skimming and curving
Out and in,
With a turn of her head,
And lift of her chin,
And a gleam of her eye,
And a twirl and a spin;
Sailing under
The breathless hush
Of the willows and back
Of the frozen rush;
Out of the island
And round the edge,
Swerving close
To the popular route,
And round the lake
On a single foot,
With a two, and a three
And a loop, and a ring;
Where Mary glides
The lake will sing!
Out in the mist
I hear her now
Under the frost,
Of the willow-bough
Easily sailing,
Light and fleet
With a song of the lake
Beneath her feet.

Carol Kemp (13) and Nicola McMaster (13)
Sheraton Comprehensive School, Stockton-on-Tees,
Cleveland

Presents

With all my presents
Wrapped and tied,
I've quite forgotten
What's inside.

When people open them
They'll be
No more surprised I think
Than me!

Melissa Bowden (8) Loxwood School, W. Sussex

In Love

We Walked and Talked

Ambling through the daisy fields,
Flowers in my sticky hands,
Shorts ending at my grazed knees,
And mud from there to my shoes,

Quietly humming to myself,
And gabbling to Miss Green,
Her answers short, but giving praise,
Made me pleased and talkative.

Me and Miss, talked as we walked,
And I thought that I was someone special,
That is until that afternoon,
When she was picked up by her lover.

Her lover did not look that old to me,
And somehow I just did not know
The difference between the two of us.
And thus my innocent jealousy set in.

Tim Weller (14) The King's School,
Canterbury, Kent

The Full and Vicious Circle

If only you knew . . .
If only I could say that single, silent-almost phrase
I have to say; but words are only breaths enlivened
And breathing all the time, I know the effect is
    momentary.

So read it in my eyes where there is no cipher to
    decode
And you will learn that yearning yearns too much, to
Crack. I smack myself
But pinch me for the reality of it and see whether I
    wince
Or sigh.

If only you realized . . .
When you brush, breathe, come either way within an
    inch
A touch becomes too much; and when the
    opportunity arises
I fingertip you as porcelain.
Crack; and the reality of contemptuous eyes would
    be fragmented,
But the pain — its splinters were, are and will be
    cherished.

If only you were serious . . .
We word one another but most we word ourselves
I hope the deception is deceiving more than me;
This urgency to have opened oyster-shell secrets,
Is only when I want you to prise apart and capture the
    pearl.

If only you would dare . . .

Sara Pennell (17) Ferndown Upper School, Dorset

In and Out of Joyce's Daydream

One and one is two,
Two and two is four,
Three and three are the times I
watched the weakness in your wandering eye waver
as lovers for the first times two kissed, without a
care.
Two times two is four,
Three times three is the smoothness of
your skin is so sublime times nine is seventy-two days
now you have gone. I wanted to tell you how I, don't
   know the answer,
miss your loving gaze.
I stare at your empty seat.

'James! 12 times 11 is 132.'
'Yes miss' you.

Darren Bowget (14) Mintlaw, Aberdeenshire

No Perfect Disguise (for A.T.)

I feel like a china doll –
Hollow, emotionless.
An image of an image
Without a soul.

But china cracks, paint peels,
So 'handle with care'.
Even for living
It's no perfect disguise.

Charlotte Cook (17) Alton College, Hants

A Time For Love

I love you

swinging	every second
wound up	ready to spring
moving	anti-clockwise
ringing	in my ears

I love you

waking	☐
working	☐
laughing	☐
drinking	☐
crying	☐
sleeping	☐
always	☐

Please tick   inside me

Anna Pegler (16) Billericay, Essex

Love So Surprise?

When in the wind is the where?
With the blue-eyes, the you-eyes,
And with the so wind in your hair
So golden, so random surprise?

Whither your lips so red,
Which meet mine in when and in where?
What words my lips so said
So lost in the random-wind there?

So love-lost in purple heather, or
Who else in the world so fair
Or cheek so smooth, or law
Of Nature surprise in the care?

When the You and the wind in the heather
With me, lips, words of Us love?
Is Nature random, so together
The Us and the so clouds above?

Is love in your eyes, You so fair?
Above us the random cloud wise?
Whither the random when and the where?
My nature – love you – so surprise?

Jon Harley (16) Barnard Castle, Co. Durham
(Highly commended)

'Spring Still Life', Richard Cobb (15)

Still Life

The promise of Heaven
A little way off
Smiles, charming, in your face,
Teasing me, ripping me from calm.

This creased Polaroid –
My god, my life, when you are away –
Picked from a moment, meaningless to you,
Holds all beauty.

Hopelessly, I am in love
With a paper image,
Jealously hidden, that it cannot be soiled
By plundering eyes seeking grace.

Roy Biddle (15) Chilworth, Southampton

The Marriage Vows
of Beatrice and Benedick
or, ' "Suffer Love!"; a good epithet.
I do suffer love indeed . . .'

Let us scrap, and weal each other's wit
With spiteful claws.
Let us scorn and scour sarcasm across each other's
   pride
With callous, careless temerity.
Let us bicker, bitch and bark
And slander sentiment, libel our love
Before it spoils, too saccharin.

Let us love each other horribly
And permit ourselves the precious luxury of hatred,
With barbed reminders of lovers' course ill-navigated.
Torment, tease and tantrum please endure,
Lest the war of words suffers to become wind-calmed,
Pitched into paradise imperfect.

Let us say we love and yet love not,
For in the paradox lies our perverse perfect.
And if in a moment we desist from our dissent
Then purer, further thrives our love;
Rarefied, yet no more artifice of ornament.

Sara Pennell (17) Ferndown Upper School, Dorset

The Next Train to Dover . . .

Brainlessly gathering the passes
Of the masses
With hypnotising monotony.
A whining screech
As the metal monster breaks
And releases its steam.

The next train to Dover?

The waves break on the shore
Rustling the pebbles on retreat.
A fizz; opening the sparkle
The delirium of buzzing scent.
The smell of her hair
Recalls a memory of a lover.

The next train to Dover?

Beginning to gather energy
Climactically spouting steam
As his blood circulates faster.
The wheels rotate heavily
Witnessing the sweet sorrow of parting.
The metal plates roll and roll.

The next train to Dover?

Rolling and turning in harmony
With the temperamental breeze.
She plucks St Peter's herb,
The Samphire in his hand –
The mystical plant
Melts into the reality of a ticket.

The next train to Dover?

Mechanically snipping the paper
Pointing to the parallel platform.
Another pulse of colourlessly clad commuters.
The constant questioning continues.
The vision obliterates all else;
Pensively gathering the passes.

The muffled memory
scarcely audible
through the megaphone
is caught and carried by the wind:

The next train to Dover . . .

Natascha Engel (17) Canterbury, Kent

Rose

Red rose, red rhythmed rose,
Red tooth-mugged ripe rhythmed rose
Is pulsing, quick, on my rose-shelf.

The room seems full of petals,
Red, red, red rose petals, and
They sing upon the floor.
My eyes, perhaps, are petals:
Red with love, pulsating: petals.

O there is a young, blush, red rose
Vivid in my tooth-mug:
                   no one has seen her
Save me:
        my eyes which, like rose's
Red eye, she brightens and bares.

James Loxley (16) Epping, Essex
(Highly commended)

'Chrysanthemums in a Teapot', Esther Grant (10)

The Family

My Prison

Better take cover,
(Well, run upstairs)
Adolf Hitler's on the prowl,
(Well, Mum's a bit angry)
I've just bombed the airplane factory,
(Well, smashed the greenhouse)
I've got to escape the bloodthirsty hounds,
(Well, my friend's poodle is staying for a while)
But I've been caught in an iron-vice grip,
(Well, my Mum's caught up)
Oh no! The prison camp is nigh,
(Well, my bedroom)
It's the filthy clangers for me,
(Well, my bedroom's a bit messy)
Two guards stand watch,
(Well, my two teddies)
Outside a fire is raging around the factory,
(Well, my Dad's angry)
Then I hear footsteps approaching,
(Well, my Mum's wearing flip-flops)
The cell door is flung open,

(Well, my sticker-covered bedroom)
The punishers step forward
(Well, my Dad could certainly be one)
I face them bravely with English pride,
(Well, hide under my bed clothes)
They carry evil torture weapons,
(Well, my Dad's hand is tensed)
They begin to interrogate me,
(Well, start to shout at me)
They place me in the electric chair,
(Well, my new beanbag)
And ask about the bombed factory,
(Well, the greenhouse)
I reply 'I will not tell!'
(Well, instead I lied)
Oh no, what's going to happen to me,
(Well, nothing hopefully)
Then the goodies arrive,
(Well, Nan's just rung the doorbell)
It's celebrations and great feasting tonight!
(Well, lovely jam doughnuts, my favourite!)

Richard Hopkins (14)
Darrick Wood School, Orpington, Kent

Pancakes

Mummy made pancakes on Tuesday
She tossed them in the air
One fell on the floor
Two fell on the chair
One fell on the cooker
One fell on the grate
But lucky me I got three
Because they fell on my plate.

Glenn O'Neill (8)
St Joseph's Primary School,
Newcastle-upon-Tyne

Mother's Day Musings

Blast Mother's day!
The costly card,
The refrigerated rose
And worst of all
The breakfast in bed
soggy sausage
burnt bacon
And scrunchy puffs,
all un-scrunchy
Blast Mother's day!

Michelle Bennett (11)
Padgate C.E. School, Warrington

Mummy's New Hat

Mummy came home from the shops one day,
With an elegant hat so dainty and gay,
It perched on her head a marvellous creation,
She felt so proud and full of elation,
Daddy thought it was so extraordinary,
I didn't think it was very ordinary.
It was red and green and purple and shaped rather
    like a mop,
It had cherries on the sides of it and a feather on
    the top.

Paula Vincent (7)
Bangor Central Primary School,
Co. Down, N. Ireland

My Dad

My dad is a policeman
He's fat and very tall
At night he checks the houses
Behind the garden wall
He looks for any robbers
That might be prowling near
While I'm in bed he keeps me safe
And drives away my fear.

Julia Hughes (6)
Tynywern Infants School,
Trethomas, Gwent

Then My Mother Began to Cry

When he came in with my mother
And sat down in the shade,
I knew what his coming meant.
But so what? Many others besides
mother have split up!
Then men say, 'Women are bad.'
And the women say there are hardly any good
husbands.
Father was so naive,
He let himself be plucked,
Like a partridge from the nest.
This other she knew how to seduce
and I'm sorry for him.
But also for mother, for she bears his child,
A child he cares little about,
He talked and talked
But what good are his fine words
When mother feels like swords are
digging into her womb.
And sharp knives cutting at her heart.
Well, she fought her two sicknesses,
The one in her heart and the one in
her body,
She swallowed her grief, all her grief,
She pasted a wide smile across her weary face
And that smile which made her ill,
told him of her contempt,
but also her forgiveness and her pity.
He left hardly turning his head –
Then my mother began to cry.

Mohammed Ashraf (15)
Sunnyside Secondary School, Halifax, W. Yorks

Gone

When's he coming back Mam?
When's he coming home?
Why's he gone away Mam,
And left us all alone?

Why didn't you make him stay Mam?
It's Christmas in two weeks
He will be back before then
He's to mend the roof, it leaks.

Yes, I know he couldn't fix it
But it doesn't matter what he does
I don't mind if the roof caves in
As long as he's here with us.

Where's his big black boots Mam?
Where's his coat and hat?
When's he coming home Mam?
When's he coming back?

Ellen Jackson (12) Bristol

Logic

Last year
My father died.
It stretched him out
And took his breath
Away clear.
It was so much it
Broke the back
Of reason.

When I find hoards
Of foreign coins,
Or see his books
And pills again,
I leave them back
And dust around those
Little jabs
Of pain.

Rosemary Cowan (17)
Co. Londonderry, N. Ireland
(Award winner)

Contrast Christmas

A sombre place, a sombre mind.
A scapegoat corner, a flippant memory.
A Christmas token, a salamander of joy.
A taken liberty, a thunderfly of consent.
A luck note given, a safe journey hoped.
A sterling note taken, another visit urged.
A fitting atmosphere, a warmth present.
A glancing air, an overpowering desire.
The first line was Grandparents.
The next, the whore.

Bruce Newsome (12)
The Hall School, Market Harborough, Leics

You Remembered

You remembered everything in the past,
Didn't you Grandad.
Things that happened a day or two ago,
You would forget about.

Like the time my mum was small –
You took her for a picnic on a hill,
And on the way home
Half way down that hill
She remembered the orange peel –
Alone and sad on a strange hill.
She dragged you back to get it.
You let her; you always did!

You remembered the war
And all the funny stories
That a sergeant major has to tell.

You said you had a private.
He was Irish
And he always polished your shoes black –
Your shoes were brown.

There were lots more stories like that.
Most of them were exaggerated.
I knew that,
But they were funny
So I said nothing.
I didn't want to hurt your feelings.

But I stopped hearing all those funny stories
On January 16th, 1981 –
The day you died!

Susie Moore (11) Borth, Dyfed
(Highly commended)

53

Granny

My Granny's had her hair done
She's had it done bright red
She's had it dyed so it will hide
The grey bits in her head

My Granny's started yoga
She wiggles on the floor
And ties herself up into knots
My Granny is no bore

My Granny's on a diet
She's stopped eating chips
And chocolate cakes and jammy buns
That put wobbles on her hips

My Granny's started swimming
She takes me to the pool
While I just flap she does front crawl
And makes me feel a fool

My Granny's really trendy
At the disco she's a wow
The problem is she seems to be
Much younger than me now!

Jill Batterley (11)
Wirksworth, Derbyshire

'Grandma', Timothy Cooper (7)

People Poems

After Adrian Mitchell –
We Liked His Stuff!

You came up from London with it.
Came into our school with it.
POETRY
We liked your stuff!

You took all your books from it
We got lots of laughs from it.
POEM BAG
We liked your stuff!

For your birthday you were given it.
Took it off when you got hot in it.
LEATHER JACKET
We liked your stuff!

Many a cat was killed by it.
Everyone was filled by it.
CURIOSITY
We liked your stuff!

All your poems are printed on it.
Some are still in scribbles on it.
PAPER
We liked your stuff!

You failed your exams for it.
Our mums and dads all danced to it.
ROCK AND ROLL
We liked your stuff!

Lines in your poems created it.
Children burst right out with it.
LAUGHTER
We liked your stuff!

Excitement in the classroom –
Ideas in our head –
Creating, thinking, writing –
We were the poets instead.
For you we created them.
Then we went away with them.
POEMS
Because we liked your stuff!

Class 9 (11)
Tyldesley County Primary School,
Wigan, Lancs

Corn Child

The child lies on his back,
Amongst the tall ears of corn
As he watches fluffy, puffy clouds,
Floating in the evening of late summer,
Across the dark blue sky,
And he hears the corn rustling,
And the birds singing in the huge trees,
Trailing his hand in the cool water,
Letting the water filter through his fingers,
And the corn becomes sea, and
The trees become Islands . . .
The other approaching person becomes
A lone survivor of a shipwreck,
Stranded miles from anywhere,
Floating on the sea. The sun once more appears
And the corn becomes visible,
And the field turns dark,
As the light fails,
And the birds put their heads
Under their wings,
The trees become silhouetted
Against far hills that loom in the cool,
Dim distance of the night . . .

David Harman (10)
The Beacon School, Amersham, Bucks
(Highly commended)

From a Railway Carriage

Slowly the station platform diminishes,
Fades into the gathering dusk,
Helped by the belching, billowing steam,
Passing by the dirty streets and houses,
Grimy men and boys returning from work,
After a hard day down the coal mines,
Garden after garden flies past,
In a flurry of smoke,
The cattle in their fields quietly go to sleep,
The sheep as well, all sink into a dark world,
A world where no one can intrude,
Over the hill a dark gaping mouth appears,
Suddenly we plunge into darkness,
The carriage sways dangerously to and fro,
In the cheerless hole,
Then a white spot appears,
We are nearing the end of the long, long journey.

Catherine Smith (10)
St Georges County Junior School, Shrewsbury, Salop

A Little Girl

Clutching an abstract jigsaw piece,
Fraying scarlet ribbons
Among hair that delights
In torturing the comb.
Her flowered apron
Patterned with orange soup stains
That seem to creep everywhere,
Like rust.
A proud chin and freckled nose,
Twitching now and then.
She delights in bold bright
And preferably noisy things!
No patience for books
Which mainly seem to be
Objects to throw around the room.
A champion cuddler,
With a passion for jelly babies
Though everyone,
Green red or black,
Gets a decent and elaborate funeral.
Dancing and prancing
Definitely a potential ballet dancer
She triumphantly lays,
The final jigsaw piece 'Mummy look!'

Jane Lumb (14) Redcar, Cleveland

The Learning Session

A cloud of invisible knowledge hangs over the heads
of the scholars.
As they, in preparation for exams, work studiously
so as to achieve their silent goals.

A busy silence.
Bustles about, from desk to desk, as papers are
    dropped,
throats are cleared, and, in weariness, a sigh is heard.

Occasionally a whisper flies cautiously across the
    room
jumping skilfully over the teacher's head, so as to
reach its destination.
A muffled laugh, and a bold giggle.
'Shh . . . h.' Then silence.

Sara Correia (15) Rotherham, Yorks

Wild Eyes

Look at her eyes
Blue above rosy cheeks
Glittering as she looks
For some new source of amusement.

What is behind her eyes?
A small child loveable as any other
Full of love and trust
As she runs to her mother

Or is there a determined spirit
With enough strength
To change the world with its wildness
Many will try to tame her
But they can only try.

Look at her eyes,
Innocent now.
But some day
A toy will not be enough for her.

June Black (14)
Loreto College, Coleraine

'Untitled', Tracy Wary (15)

My Friend's Head

In it there is a romance story,
Screams, plots and double plots,
A liquidizer full of younger brother.

In it there's a Jekyll and Hyde,
An assassination attempt on the next-
door neighbour,
To stop him singing in the bath.
There's a triangular prism,
Turning slowly,
Soft pink shapes,
Giant marshmallows,
A sandy beach,
A Sherman tank,
An acid bath full of teachers.

Katy Senior (14)
Pudsey Grangefield School, Leeds

School

Bang! Slap! Punch!
Those two are having a fight.
One of them swings a nice left hook
The other swings a right.
The teacher comes to stop the fight
And accidentally takes the right.

Patrick McCoy (12) Bagshot, Surrey

The Loser

Anger in her eyes, the ultimate hate,
Fury and passion on her face
Watching the others
Only seeing who does not care,
Oblivious of who does.
Looking with disbelief at them as they leave her.
Humiliation fills her.
Rage and shame.
Someone trying to comfort her
To persuade her it's not worth her rage.
She could not have won anyhow.
But she is blind to consolations
Filled only with bitter disappointment.

Ann Tanner (9)
Aboyne Primary School, Aberdeenshire

'School Dinners' Craig Mills (12)

A Schoolboy Hero

Rows of little boys line up in a corridor,
Like stretched fishing line they stand,
Taut, tense and silent, but for the occasional kink,
In the form of an unwittingly conspicuous whisper
Or a giggle. Wearing authority like a tight collar,
The monitors stand, or pace, occasionally stopping
And correcting a kink. 'Go and wash your hands',
'Comb your hair – it's awful.' At this, the small eyes
Are lifted up reluctantly and momentarily they catch
The eyes of the false God.
Then they return their sojourn to the floor
And the silence is broken by footsteps,
The gush of water, and the noise of a towel on a rail.
The boy returns to the queue,
The monitor strides away, smiling conceitedly
At his small exercise of authority.
Many eyes follow him, reading his smile,
Misinterpreting it. Subconsciously they note
Anything he does, later to copy it
In their own movements.
For everything he does is right –
He is the hero.

Luke Dunn (14) The King's School, Canterbury, Kent

'Tough As Old Boots', Nicholas Brady (15)

The Local Gang

In walked the local gang
Forming a huge semi-circle,
A pathetic facade.
Total pretence
They glanced around
People stared,
They glared,
Smirks across their faces
Deep down they were scared
They stood there
Shoulders back chests out
Hoping to look tough.

Rachael Waddington (13)
Shipley, W. Yorks

Scene in Winter

The girl stands at the window shivering slightly:
Wrapped in a warm towel, she looks to the East
And the sunrise.
She hears the wind
Tearing the trees and buffeting the walls of the house.
She sees the wind
Carving mysterious shapes in the snow –
Soft, smooth, delicate shapes that
Suddenly, like an unsuspected twist of speech
Taper to a knife edge – harsh, and cruel, and cold.
Glancing at the hills above where the trees' branches
    bend and sway,
The girl sighs and turns into the room.

Claire Dickinson (15) Alton Convent, Hants

The Blaze Is Over

The inferno has left its toll.
A mountain of deep grey ashes lie like snow.
Burnt out memories of coloured lights line the way.
Now the lights that danced across the sky like chariots
Are only present in a child's thoughts.
The night before dreams had come alive,
As small children beheld the fairy rain.
The coloured sparks descended like stars from a
    magician's gown.
For the small children the night had been an
    enchanted fairy-tale,
As make-believe came true.

The whole sky lit up like Aladdin's cave,
Each child's eyes lingered on a passing ray of light.
The sky was a stage, alight with dancing performers.
Each act brought something fresh and new.
The night seemed never ending.
The sky a fabric of coloured hue.
But not today, the air is silent.
Only a child's memory keeps the magic burning.

Ann Marie Evans (15) Owston Ferry, Doncaster

An Eye

An eye looks at me in a shop,
Scanning me round checkouts,
Through clothes hangers
An eye,
Searching, searching for something, someone,
Yet I do not know who or what.
The eye, fixed to a dome-like face,
Yet no face can be seen.
Nearby, a box with a screen
Shows my face to everyone.
Suddenly another face appears
Looking conscious of itself,
That face belongs to a person.
He picks up an object,
Runs away.
All over the shop bells, buzzers and bleepers
Send a shrill alarm.
The camera has struck.

Thomas Bazeley (10)
County J. and I. School, Bradford-on-Avon, Wilts

The Outsider

The teacher sat at the front of the class,
Not two yards
From her teenage pupils,
Only a few years apart.

But they greeted her words,
So hopefully uttered,
With sneers and moans
And whispers and groans
And snorts and giggles
And coughs and sniggers.

They rejected her essays,
Scorned her ideas,
Laughed at her flares,
Made fun of her ears.

Oh, but not once
Did they misbehave,
Leave the classroom,
Or disobey.
When she asked for silence
They gave it;
With yawns and glances at watches.
When told to get on
They got on alright;
Long boring essays
Minus imagination.
When told to bring in
An article of interest
For all the class to enjoy,
They merely forgot.

She tried so very hard.

But when they stopped laughing,
Chatting and whispering,
Their faces became blank.
Minds flitted to loved ones,
To Saturday's disco,
To new outfits,
To No. 1.

She pleaded, bribed, shouted and cried,
And they smiled and tapped their heads
Behind raised folders.
And as her confidence trickled away,
They made sarcastic comments.
'Have you always had a stutter?'

And so she gave,
Gave them private reading,
Didn't even try
To be understood
Or listened to,
To be allowed in.

Why didn't she set them essays?
What about their 'O' levels?
'This isn't English,'
The kids complained.
'If we fail,' they shouted,
'It'll all be your fault.'

Emily Wilson (13)
Sidcot School, Winscombe, Avon

The Drug Addict

Through visions of fear they pass
And for a moment they are released
They experience
New colour, new sound, new beauty
The fourth dimension
And as it lasts, they live in hope.
But the journeys are shorter each time,
And the price is hard to pay.
And each time they return
The world is a little greyer.

Zoë Crompton (14) Cheltenham, Glos

The Nose

Once there was a person
Who didn't like his nose
So he went into the garden
He sprayed it with the hose.
The nose went red
He went to bed
I think I like my nose
Now, he said.

Mark New (7)
Overdale Infants School,
Leicester

A Meeting with Madness
(for Mr W.)

You rooted out the innocence
Buried deep within me;
Desperate as some drowning man
Your need to cling
Fed courage
To your impotency.

I smiled; not without pity,
Sensed the struggle of your words;
The random catalogue, crisis-strewn,
A life shown etched
Not written
Through the red-worn web of nerves.

You tried to offer blindly
A sensation scarcely there;
Your life destroyed by accident
Misplaced your faith
In friendship
And fresh wounds are harsh to bear.

I gained your trust, encouraged it;
Threw caution to the wind;
Realizing that with sweet pretence
You could derive
Strange sanity
Deceiving your warped mind.

Charlotte Cook (17)
Alton College, Hants

Encounters of the Suburban Kind

Mrs Amelia Bodfrey, the everyday suburban
     housewife
Performing the chores
Or so it seems . . .

The children safely tucked up in bed for the night
No one about
The transformation begins.
Her skin peels to wrinkles;
     From her clean hands cats' claws take shape,
     Warts appear here and there;
The finishing touches to a nightmare.

The evil sorceress collects her hat and cloak
Calls her cat, Maugrim, to her side,
And glides quietly out of the window
In the dark night sky, she joins
Black silhouettes of cloaks swirling, swirling.

Mrs Amelia Bodfrey
Arrives at a forest clearing
Unknown to human kind,
Other witches descend,
The wind howls like an omen,
It knows what abominations are in store,
Repulsive rituals take place;
Sacrifices are offered up in honour of the mighty
Head Wizard Gogron.
The nightmarish chanting growing
LOUDER and LOUDER still!
This is the climax of the witches' assembly!

The first trace of dawn appears,
The witches depart as quickly as they came.

Next morning,
Mrs Amelia Bodfrey
Greets her children, slightly ruffled
No sign of the encounters of the night.

But if you look closely
You can see the gleam of her cats' eyes . . .

Linda McKendrick (10)
St Andrew's Primary School, Falkirk

Our Flo

One day our Flo, who was rather large
Gave up eating bread and marge.
And she said to her brother Jim
'One day I will be rather thin.'
She used to curve in most odd places
But began to hold up her skirt with braces.
Yet this was not enough for Flo,
So to 'Keep Fit' she began to go,
And jogging around the park each day
To all her friends she began to say
'This dieting is good for me,'
Then have a yoghurt for her tea.
But one day, when she got a pain,
Our poor Flo fell down the drain.
The moral of this story's true:
Dieting too much isn't good for you.

Christy Haworth (10)
St James C.E. Primary School,
Blackburn, Lancs

Loud Future

Listen to deafness with an open mind
Think before you mouth your ugly words,
To cover embarrassing silence.
'Don't blame her', they say,
But respect and equality
Is the push that brings her forward.
A criticism is not a sin,
It's kinder than a smile,
Full of ignorance and sympathy.

Don't trap her in the ugly duckling caste,
Always wondering what went wrong.
This swan is growing with the trees,
She makes mistakes like you and me.
Her mind is a kaleidoscope of sound,
Ready to explode on an unknowing world.
Every observation filed,
Every colour collected.
The screams emerge as tears,
Her heartbeat grows in fiery eyes
As a finger dials a number.
Full of confidence,
A hopeful buzz,
But the line falls cold and dead.
World, keep trying to understand.

Julie Sherriff (15)
Longlands School, Stourbridge, W. Midlands

'Tea For Two?'

An old rocking chair,
To and fro it rocks,
A small figure
Sits quietly
With the flames of a fire
For company
The crinkled specs
On his nose
Slide slowly down.
A whistle of a kettle,
'Tea for two?'
He says,
'Sugar for you?'
He wishes he could say those words
In front of someone.
He sits down
And recalls
The lost memories
Of far-off days.

Glyn Robinson (10)
Park Farm C.P. School,
Folkestone, Kent

Wednesday 16th January

As time goes by
My movements are stooped
but my face holds the flicker
of a candle.
As the clock ticks I sit silently
in my chair of thoughts.

My fingers are bony from
my life of work
I remember when I was young
my face was dazzling and
my movements were merry.
As the clock ticks I sit silently
in my chair of thoughts.

The light in me has disappeared
and will never be found.
As the clock ticks I sit silently
in my chair of thoughts.

Marie Chambers (9)
Claypool C.P. School,
Horwich, Lancs

'A Man's Face', Lindsay Pearce (3) (Highly commended)

The Boxer

The great iron figure crouches,
Scabs like flowers on his knees,
And his chest is like a mountain
And his legs are thick   as trees.

He spits blood like a cherub
In a fountain spouting foam,
Ringed around by swinging ropes
And punters going home.

Broken-knuckled, shiny-eyed,
Battered, bruised, and wet
With droplets like cold rubies,
And laced with bitter sweat.

He crouches in a corner
In his pool of sparkling red
And dreads the jeers which soon will fall
Like blows upon his head.

Emma Payne (16) Hackney, London
(Award winner)

Early Swim

The night cracks,
and dawn
spills out on the water

The river bubbles;
A white limb flashes somewhere,
down in the darkness,
it sinks like a stone,
and silence hangs, like death,
over the black water

As brown reeds tangle
with blond hair,
a flower bends
and drops its heavy petals
over the surface;
white eyes stare out of the depths

Suddenly the surface explodes
into droplets; lungs
gasp for air,
and pale arms grab for the bank

A bird in the weeping willow
bursts into wild song

Emma Payne (16) Hackney, London
                    (Award winner)

The Day The Workmen Arrived

On Monday morning the men arrived,
With an old blue van parked in the drive.
Picks and shovels and an old green tent,
A yellow machine for mixing cement,
Buckets and hammers and red and white poles,
Ladders and spades and wire in rolls.
One at the door for a while had knocked.
There was no one in and it wasn't locked,
So into the house went this happy mob
And soon began to get on with the job.
Doors came off and the bath went out,
A gutter was changed and so was a spout.
Cupboards went up quick as a wink,
The once blue kitchen was soon painted pink.
A nice stone fireplace which looked quite new
Had to be shifted as it would do.
Then into the drive came a well-dressed man
Waving some papers in his hand
'Stop,' he cried, 'what a terrible mess!'
'I'm afraid you've come to the wrong address.'
The man in charge looked up with a frown
And as he did the ceiling came down.

Lorraine Woods (11)
Millington Primary School, Portadown, N. Ireland

Philistine, Reprise

An empty tear, wells. Becomes

Odysseus' ocean of solitude with
Cresting cry of . . . sirens.

An enisled mind chills the
Lapping sorrows of dun waters.
Albescent, the ocean becomes
Desert. Dunes stir silently where
Waves once broke spirits.

He fears to tread where

Footprints betray his path, and
Uncertainty follows, follows . . .

Let Hagar's son, Ishmael,
Come from beyond the veil,
Then he to Jericho, will go
And laugh. Until the walls
Shiver, sunder, and fail.

Simon Coughlan (17)
Exeter, Devon

Icarus

I saw him in the sky
Cutting through the wind like a razor.
A hot beam of sun caught his wing
Rushing to the earth
Unlike a bird
Streaming from the heavens in a mad flame.

Massimo Franco (13)
Mill Vale Middle School, Dunstable, Beds

Suzanne

'A Pirate', Suzanne Gair (5)

Smugglers

The sea is calm tonight,
The silver moon slips between ghostly grey clouds
unrolling a rippling carpet of light towards the shore
at Port Ronald where I stand.

The sleeping shadows of rocks lie curled
round pools as still as glass.
Pebbles rustle in the gentle tide
and whispering waters wash the shore.

And if I listen carefully I can almost hear
the sounds of centuries ago.
The sails fluttering faintly out on the bay
and oars splashing softly as the boat pulls near.

The sweet smell of brandy in its wooden casks,
Distant voices muttering as eyes search the shore
For the watchers waiting
with bobbing lanterns winking in the dark.

Gone forever, they are here no more
As I stand alone on the Port Ronald shore.

Debbie Church (9) St Patrick's School, Troon, Ayrshire
(Highly commended)

Gossips

'Have you heard this?' asked the woman
who had watched the birth of Christ
through a crack in the wall.
'She had her man to help her!
Have you ever heard anything as disgusting as that?'

'And then guess what happened, some shepherds
    came.
Imagine anything as silly as that –
all them shepherds leaving their sheep, just to see a
    baby!
I thought it was daft.'

'You won't believe this:
three kings coming all the way
from beyond Jerusalem to Bethlehem
just for a new-born baby!
Well, I think it's stupid, don't you?'

'Yes, I do, because
do you know what happened while you were
    shopping?'
'No, what?'
'Well I was watching and you know what these Kings
    were about?'
'Yes, go on.'
'Well, they were giving presents to the baby:
    one was gold, but I don't know what the other two
        were.'
'Now this is stupid – who would give a baby gold?'

'I know. And the shepherds gave the baby – er –
I forgot, but it was a sheep or a goat,
I know it was one of them.
You won't believe this at all:
I heard them praising God
and heard them talk about seeing angels.'

'Well, I saw it.'
'How much did you see?'
'The same. I think they are all crackpots.
Goodbye.'
'I agree with you.
Goodbye.'

Mark Godfrey (13)
Northways Special School, Wetherby, W. Yorks.

The Ghost

I am the candle of light.
I draw air from the breath of a newly born robin.
I am like the yellow, burnt pages of a disused Bible.
I am like the hands of a globe, I steer my way towards
    the end of eternity.
I move like the waves of dried grass drawn
Up in a howl of wind.
I am different, I live in a different atmosphere.
I am like a curled cat perched high in the swaying
    trees, watching the roots
Of the world gradually wither.

Piers Shepperd (13) Taunton, Somerset

Building

Steel . . . suspended above
Silver oceans of tin-can pollution
And oil-slicked dirt.
Strong, permanently sturdy.
The men tormented by
The gale-force
by the cold.

One man a tool.
A single vulnerability –
Hung high from a white,
                    white
                        cloud.

A rope –
a gallowing crane.
Clanking slates,
swearing shouts,
swaying slopes –
'Pass the parcel' metal bars.

The whizz, the drill, the slam,
the crush . . .
Man-made muscle –
pile upon pile upon pile upon
. . . pile

Clockwork nervousness –
Constant brave.
Teamwork – keep at it – nod,
to the foreman
once in every while.

Awaited buzzing of a shift change
Step back in admiration
but don't fall off its edge –
Your work,
your priceless effort . . .
eternally,
skylined,
concrete
bridge.

Maxine Harfield (14)
The Crestwood School,
Eastleigh, Hants

Hands

Stealing, killing
Wicked hands
Wretched, terrible
Cruel hands.
Slapping, punching
Naughty hands.
Bad hands,
Bad hands.

Praying, helping,
Kind hands.
Clapping, shaking,
Friendly hands.
Patting, giving,
Loving hands.
Good hands,
Good hands.

Clare Brooks (6)
Pentlepoir C.P. School, Kilgetty, Dyfed

Mark's Story

No ordinary captive this –
No peasant drunk on Passover wine,
    No petty thief.
There was a great crowd in the Garden,
Torches, the smoke rising to the starlit sky
Like unquiet spirits, bathed the Olive trees
    With golden light.
No ordinary captive would inspire so many,
Create sparks of fire in the eyes of priests,
Let crowds bawl their curses, their mockery to
    his face,
        Yet remain silent.
I will never forget that face – so strained
And pale – a mask of death, in which the eyes
Burned like flames of fire – so deep and
    profound as to know
        All of life, and beyond.
He needed no army to fetch him away –
A ragged, long-haired peasant – he had done no
    harm,
And yet he let their rough hands push him, herd
  him, while he,
    More powerful than any, did nothing to prevent
    them.
        They said I belonged to him too,
But I denied it – they ripped my clothes –
I ran from them naked, into the night, and in the
    mantle of darkness,
        I hide my face.
It was only then that I did know him –
The man the crowds loved, who healed the sick –

Now betrayed by the same men who only a
     week ago
          Had heralded his arrival.
    I had betrayed him too –
Ran away from his face and hid myself, and in the
    bitter realization,
          I turned my head away, bowed low in shame,
          And my eyes were wet with tears.

Sara Jane Ratheram (14) Harborne, Birmingham
(Highly commended)

The Dancer

Suddenly,
In the glare of the spotlight the dancer appears,
Head poised
His body tense and alert,
Beauty of line and form,
From head to toe
A flash of muscle
Reflecting power, calmness
And flexibility of movement
Suddenly he surges upwards
His controlled movement and pent-up energy
Conveying thoughts and emotions
Love, hatred, joy and sorrow,
All captured in his expressive body
An instrument of communication.

Rachael Millward (13)
Nabwood Middle School, Shipley, W. Yorks

The Life and Times of Thomas Becket: A Tale Must I Tell . . .

A tale must I tell,
A tale of deceit, of betrayal,
Of a man, pale of skin, tall of stature,
Of a priest, so turbulent, so pious,
A menace to my king and realm.
An unfortunate year, 1118,
Such a person brought forth,
That clever, deceitful man,
Whose winning, stuttered speech
Won friendship of King Henry.
A friendship undeserved,
A friendship ephemeral.
What saw my liege in such an ugly man?
His nose so prominent,
The mark of a traitor.
For nine treacherous years,
Beside his royal person,
Stood that man, his chancellor,
Thomas of Becket, then witty, then gay.
Harmonious was their work,
Successful, their hunts.
But, this ill-begotten friendship could not last.
His majesty, the king
A decision did make,
And Becket, chose he,
As Archbishop of Canterbury.
And that play actor,
Upon his own private stage,
No longer the role required
Of chancellor of great charisma.

So away were cast his worldly pleasures.
His love of festivities forgotten,
His excessive energy subdued.
Away were cast his kingly robes,
Tunics and cloaks, apparel of the past.
And upon the stage, there strut
A pious priest with frugal life.
Alas, ne'er was cast away
His strength of character,
His alertness, his deceit.
Oh no, these bloomed and thrived,
And forth came
Thomas, Archbishop of Canterbury,
That turbulent priest.
But woe, alas!
Now stood he not for king.
Precedence in the Church, there lay.
Dared he to betray King Henry's trust,
When at a meeting, stood he up,
That troublesome priest,
And dared defend rights
Of criminous clerks!
Dared oppose my liege's decision!
Dared justify the system of sanctuary!
Why, when all had rightly spoken,
Did he, alone, disagree?
What holds the guilty clergyman
Above the guilty common man?
A peasant burns upon a stake,
Whilst a deacon, his mild punishment receives,
His benefit of clergy.
And as for those hounds who flee
From law and order,

Why should they, on holy ground, sanctuary seek?
Nor is this an account,
His wrongs to justify,
For, dissatisfied, too, was he,
That without consent of Henry,
No church courts could visit Rome.
So Henry's eyes,
Bloodshot with anger became,
His fiercy countenance unleashed,
Upon he who disagreed.
And upon a chill and windy night,
Across the channel, Becket fled,
To refuge in France.
No amount of intervention
Brought about reconciliation.
But, although in refuge, still, was Becket,
Henry, Prince was crowned.
Enraged at this was Becket,
This violation of his rights.
So stormed he back to England,
And suspended all the bishops,
Who, in the ceremony, part had taken.
But soon, King Henry word received,
And in a moment of fury, shouted,
'Will no one me rid
Of this turbulent priest?'
No sooner had those
Fatal words been uttered,
Than through the streets, there marched
Four greedy, armour-clad men.
Each sure footstep, nearer to their goal.
Each such footstep led by vision of splendour.
For to rid their king and realm
Of such a serious traitor,

A good and lawful act would be,
An act to earn great riches,
Their reward from the king.
Then rose before them, Canterbury Cathedral,
All doors barred.
But this ne'er swayed
Those greedy knights,
Who turned aside and reached
A small, wooden doorway,
No hindrance to their quest.
At once, within, is shattered
That almost tangible silence, which prevailed.
And all in an instant,
Not just the smell
Of burning incense,
But the stench of blood,
Hung in the air.
All was confusion.
Scattered were the priests and deacons,
The serried ranks, abandoned.
And soon, all, from the church, had fled,
All but Thomas, Archbishop of Canterbury,
Who resisted all efforts,
His escape to assist.
Who, but a madman, would cling to a pillar,
Inviting his assailants to easy murder?
Who but a madman, after all his treachery,
Would claim to be
No traitor to the king?
And received he, those fatal blows.
Not with his hand did he oppose.
And in his church,
There spilled his blood.
Perhaps, wished he to die?

Then left those knights, Canterbury Cathedral,
And calm prevailed, once more,
Within his haven, which betrayed him,
Although the peace of realm was shattered.
Then upon the scene,
There stepped a servant,
Henry's message, carried he,
'Stop, ye ignorant knights,
Kill ye not the Archbishop of Canterbury!'
But, mark ye, therein lay the irony,
For in death, even as in life,
Mocked he my liege,
For like an outcry from the grave,
His death, upon Henry and his realm,
Havoc wrought!

Moensie Rossier (11) Rossett, Clwyd

The Life in a Day of James Riley

SCENE THREE
*James is looking at his reflection in a mirror
hung upon a wall.*

James: The shadow of a man,
Pictured in glass,
Stone still,
As if in death,
But alive,
So alive.
Hatred's reflected
In those frosty eyes

And gone
The sparks of fire
That glint and spread
Like sunlight through a crystal
Not twenty-five,
But older,
So much older.

A ballad's
Softly sung in frosty eyes
And in sweet poetry's
Conveyed
That life's been cruel
To me.
There's sorrow
Woven in this face
The sordid tapestry
Of life,
Hung suspended
Like a star
In time,
So little time,
To fulfil those dreams
Of younger days
When black is
Black
And white is
White
And there are no shades of grey.

These frosty eyes
That see and don't forget
The shadows
On hills

The rich vibrancy
Of daffodils
Inspire the mind
With pictures
Of a world
Outside my captive cell
Time frozen still
Inside this cage
And with no time
Death's no enemy
To me.

The shadow of a man
pictured in glass,
Not alone,
For in the mind
An echo of a whisper
That reminds
Time's passing,
Always moving,
Remember James
Just one chance
And this is your life.

Joanna West (14)
Cherney School,
Headington, Oxford

A Mask?

The ballerina flitting round the stage
Gives a false impression of
A beautiful graceful girl,
Showered by fans, flowers, letters,
Graciously signing photographs or
programmes or
bus tickets or
sweet wrappers and
Retiring to a country house
To read about Pavlova or sew sequins onto dresses.
For all I know, she could be an ugly old woman,
Skinny, hiding behind the make-up.
She could be crotchety, burning her letters in the
    envelopes,
A modern 'Miss Havisham'.
Or she could be a sophisticated woman.
Looking down her nose at her adoring fans.
Going to the nearest house to eat caviare and drink
    champagne,
And feed her lap-dog with the same, but
Somehow I always come back to the beautiful, young
    girl,
Flitting round the stage.

Fiona O'Neill (13) Cookstown, Co. Tyrone, N. Ireland

The Places Where We Live

Where I Live

Smells from the distant chippy
    drift across the weary sky.
Drunks waltz down the road
at a steady stumbling pace.
The dashing trees
    sway in time to the wind.
Train hooters sound like whistling kettles.
Feather-like leaves float down
      from the moonlit sky,
        like boats
          sinking into the sea,
    then all is quiet
until an owl gives a friendly hoot
      then silence . . . !
But not for long . . .
A motorbike glides through the air at a
     horrific speed
  and then the night
      turns itself inside out.

Michael McGarvey (11) Retford, Notts

'Cottage Landscape'. Natalie Balmond (17)

Yorkshire

Flint walls cuts
the puckered land,
Crag houses have splintered and thrust up
out of the dark earth,
they squat uneasily on the hillsides

A countryside of bog and moor,
mist and drizzle,
Its people rise up
out of ditches
and its slow heart beats
in the roots of the damp heather

Emma Payne (16) Hackney, London
(Award winner)

Death of the Steel Works

Thud, bang, clash, roar,
Thud, bang, clash, roar,
Rollers humming,
Trucks chugging,
Bright lights flashing,
Hot steel hissing,
Thud, bang, clash, roar.

Tap, tap, whizz,
Tap, tap, whizz.
Taps in the office,
Hissing in the towers,
The roar of water,
The bubble of iron,
Tap, tap, whizz.

Tumble, tumble, roar,
Tumble, tumble, roar,
Coal-tipping trucks,
Empty their loads in a rush,
Intensive heat hoards the furnace,
Red hot coke burns up to the surface,
Tumble, tumble, roar.

Alas, these sounds are heard no more,
No footsteps leaving the mill,
CLOSED is the sign upon the door,
Now all is quiet and still.

Caroline Lamb (10)
Delves Lane Junior School,
Consett, Co. Durham

Night Sight

The dark muffled figure makes his secret way
   through the streets,
Swamped in a bulky grey overcoat,
The hidden lamps shed foggy spheres of shifting light,
         And the figure moves on.

A stray cat starts at the clatter of a falling dustbin lid,
       Then makes its furtive retreat,
The feline form writhing and undulating as it goes
   under a fence;
        And the figure moves.

The cruel rain pounds on the cobbled alleys,
A drenched mouse scuttles hither, thither,
The dull factory tower billows out its last breath of
   phantasmal smoke,
The figure hesitates; but then moves on.

The grey-eyed moon smiles mercifully on the scene,
      It seems to wink –
A swish, as of an angel wing, and the hoot of an owl,
   are heard.
       The figure hurries on.

A bright light flashes from a tiny square window,
A door opens – a joyful man emerges,
Happy faces, dancing, mirth and joy –
       The figure hurries on
       And enters . . .

Francis Garcia (13)
St Andrew's School, Horsell, Surrey

Fireside Visions

I look into the fire and see
A viper's tongue, dread enemy.
As quick, it licks upon the wood
Where nails like bony fingers stood.
But now are fell, midst glowing ash.
The relic's of a fire's match.

A hiss, a spit, the embers fall
From fairy residences tall.
And on the hearth they slowly die
Like comets fallen from the sky
Like luminous hands upon a clock
Helpless, they lie as others mock.

But wait — they too will have their turn
They too will fall, though now they burn.
When Midnight strikes they will have died
And Silence will herself preside
In this room, though the shadows fall
Still, here upon the bare, white walls.

Melanie Barnes (13)
Bentley Wood School, Stanmore, Middx

The After-School

Memory echoes children's voices –
Fading
– Footsteps in the dark.
Fire doors locked.
Moths flitter against invisible glass.
The school,
Is dead to the voice of the night.
But glints in the moonlight.
The classrooms are silent,
Blackboards bare.
Mice are in the dark hall,
Scavenging
Searching.
Oh sad school, slowly waiting –
For a sunrise, cock-crow
A hop-skip and jump.
Gravel in the yard crunches.
The wind whispers to you.
Windows closed as eyes close.
You're dreaming softly
Snoring.
There's taps dripping – water wasted.
You're quiet like a baby.
But cry to yourself,
Tomorrow's another day.

Andrew Wilson (14) Runcorn, Cheshire

Haunted House

Just down the road
There is a
             house
With two doors
        One
             back
        one front
With a rockery.
   Very weedy that it is
Because it is haunted.
   Always dark
Because it is a ghostly place.
It's not the right place
        For me.

Kate Lancaster (7)
Moore County Primary School,
Warrington, Cheshire

Dockland

In the man is the boy
Who thundered on short legs,
Snorting and sniffing,
Down to Dockland

To banging, rattling land's edge,
Peopled by men with muscles like great chains
Binding their arms, and voices like hammers;
To splinters and sawdust and rotten fruit
Oozing brown; to brutal cobbles and broken crates
And slated, gaping windows, and brawls and
    shouting
In the shipyards, howling saws and curling wood,
And the black, stinking puddles of sea water
Which rotted the iron anchors

Among tall ships and screaming birds the seed was
    sown:
As he sits, pinstriped, at his desk, eyes on the clock,
His longing unfolds inside him like a huge sail,
Mentally he runs up a wooden gangplank
Onto a departing ship.

Emma Payne (16) Hackney, London
(Award winner)

Atlantic Beach

It stretches out in
Summer; a white-gold
Band of loving and
Promise of sun.
The clean grit feeling
Of familiar sand
In every fold of rug
And body. The noise
Seems false, rising out
On mirage airbeds.
Little cat waves lap
Up the children,
Oiled, heavy heat
Takes a living sap.

Only the banshee
Gulls scream true. In dim
Winter dawns a face
Pock-marked by joggers'
Heels just too fast or
Slow for fluid grace.
And quiet men walk with
Dogs to Barmouth in
Flurry of salt and
Fur. Sea binds the land
In grey-blue serge, seams
White, split by the rocks,
I sit with stick
And stir my dreams.

Rosemary Cowan (17)
Co. Londonderry, N. Ireland
(Award winner)

Summer in England

Summer in England, how I remember
The deep, clear, ice-blue sky;
Sunbeams filtered through fresh green leaves
The glossy rhododendrons splashed with purple
    blooms.

The gurgle of the fountain dancing in the pond,
The gentle click of croquet, in play on the lawn;
The strenuous creak of the cumbersome branch
As the swing sways softly to and fro.

Heavy scent of honeysuckle drifting in the breeze
The smooth, moist surface of the full carafe;
Soft, springy moss enveloping your feet,
Growing thick under leaf-burdened willows.

Rebecca Harker (12)
St Catherine's School, Bramley, Surrey

Perception

As I watch the Amazonian sun slowly descend,
Closing to the world her one Cyclopean, ruby eye
And watch the silent, ancient mountains, dark as
night,
Silhouetted against the bleeding sky:
Then I am subdued;
And believe that all Life's Ishmaelite wanderings
Are but an illusion;
That greed, vengeance, hatred and man's confusion
Are nothing but echoes in the dark labyrinths of the
    mind;
And as I close my weary eyes, I find
That sleep to death must be the closest friend
And that with both life's nightmares always end.

Rachel Jagger (17) Leek, Staffs

'Richmond Street, Penzance', Bruce Le Grange (17)
(Highly commended)

A Day by the Sea

A sea of acid.
Forever.
An endless promenade.
Cold, cutting wind.
Raining
Wet.
Quick music, slow dance.
'Dance lover, dance.'

Stringy grass stands still.
Earth patches,
Bald.
Old man laughs disturbingly
Quietly.

Lapping water laps.
Slap.
Grey cliffs groan.
The weight of humanity,
Sagging.

'My naïve and sentimental friend,
I see you.'

Clouds scudding.
Black and white.
Hiding the sun.

'Come, come,' said the fox.
'You shall see yourself.'

Puddles.
Mud, mixing salty tears.
Mirrors.
Life reflected, mind entrapped.
Going now,
Bus to catch.

Peter Morris (16) Harlow, Essex

Siberia

Deep in the Arctic Circle
Where the wild, wild winds roar,
The night lasts all day long,
And in the murk the hungry lupines howl.
Across the endless plains
The eternal wastes of Siberia far into Mongolia.
Natives cling to the earth
Hardened by unchanging frost
And hollow in their hovels,
They wrap their sheepskins
Round their bodies, skin upon skin to keep at bay
The bitter frost,
A tough breed of men, they are accustomed to cold
    comfort
and twilight life.
And overhead the stars look down and mirror
The distant ice, as howls the wind
And whines the fox, far from the crowds of city life
    and light.

Lucretia King (11)
National Junior C.E. School, Grantham, Lincs

Tierra del Fuego

In the land of fires
I found a snake that swallows you
and spits out your bones.

In the land of fires
I found a woman with great strength,
She could pull a tree from the ground.

In the land of fires
I found the ghosts of explorers
who had gone there long ago.

In the land of fires
I found a giant merman
who was as tall as the Empire State Building.

In the land of fires
I found a group of cannibals
who painted life-like pictures of you
burning on a fire.

In the land of fires
I found a giant black panther
with one big eye in the middle of his forehead.

Paul Harmer (9) Rye, E. Sussex

Birds
and Beasts

The Snow-Goose

A flutter in the reeds
As the flood tastes the marshes,
And from the sharp-edged grass,
Frost-frozen in the night, the snow-goose flaps.

The hoarfrost cracks, and is swallowed
In sponges of muddy moss,
As a flurry of soft feathers
Sink into the tide-soaked tufts.

A low whistle behind the brakes
And the eager panting of spaniel;
The snow-goose rises jerkily
In a sleep-stained panic of movement.

'Bittern', Debra Rogers (14)

He spirals upwards, and hears
The silent click of a trigger.
Then a long cry as he plummets
Wildly like a melted corkscrew.

Catherine Skinner (16) Hitchin, Herts.
(Highly commended)

115

The Kestrel

At half-past five, I closed the door of a sleeping
    country inn,
Careful not to break the silence, which,
In its perfection,
Was as delicate as the bones of a young bird.

Crossed a field of wheat,
Awoken from the early morning slumber
By a gentle breath of wind.

Through the forest, on a path defined
By many walkers' feet.
The trees, so tall and old, held, indefinably, majesty
Without pride.
Their trunks were dead; the branches and leaves
    given life
By wind.
A tree had fallen, as if flicked by some unseen,
    almighty hand,
Tired of it.
As last upon the grassy plain where the castle stood.
Ancient, it was true, abandoned many, many years
before.
Decay was king, seated on a throne of moss,
And weed, and crumbling stone.
Entering where a door had been,
A banqueting hall you'd once have seen
Long ago.
I climbed the stairs most carefully, for stone
So old
Is never what it seems.
Sat on the wall the stairway ran along,

Looked at my watch; six o'clock
It said, inauspiciously
Heralding the arrival.
The kestrel appeared;
A brown speck over the distant treetops.
Approaching, it became clearer: like a huge,
    pulsating heart,
The wings beat, slowly.
The beauteous grace of the flight both
Invited, and yet prohibited comparison
With any man-made artefact.
With the grace a creature of the wild alone can
    possess,
The kestrel gently dived and landed,
Close to me along the wall.

He turned his head to face me;
I stared into his deep brown eyes,
Neither of us spoke.

At last, when convinced I was there not to harm,
But to observe,
The kestrel flew again.

Looking back from the edge of the forest,
I opened my eyes.
Dew lay, like many angels' tears,
The clouds as if they'd sighed;
As if they knew Mankind was doomed,
And in the knowing, cried.

Andrew Cowper (13)
Springfield County Middle School,
Walton-on-Thames, Surrey

The Whistlers

Silence invades the marshes
Choking all life.
Only the crackle of water on mud
Remains
And the murmur of a lazy tide
laps the estuary.
Winter sun dissolves in a brackish pool,
Lends life and colour to the inanimate
And mud moulds foam with decaying sunlight.

A harsh wail springs from the marshes,
Shrill and plaintive above the silence
And the shapelessness
Lost in the marsh grass, a seaman or soldier or marsh
    bird
And the whistlers return, cutting the silence
But desolation makes no answer.

The whirring of wings approaches and six black dots
Move rapidly across the pond's auburn horizon.
Coming eastward out of the sun
And six shrill cries echo across the mudlands,
Searching for the survivor,
Returned from exile
They draw closer and their wings shadow the
    landscape.
Orange headcrests glowing through the half-light
Larger than legend, their wings punch the skyline.

A clatter of motion and the exile explodes from the
    marsh
Mudland moans and shrinks away.
As seven huge time lords unite
Seven wails banish silence
And the great birds circle the marshlands,
Leaving Eastwards,
Vanishing into dusk.

And I shudder and turn away,
As one last bugle-like wail sears silence in two
And light deserts time.

Karen Haysom (17) Billericay School, Essex

(This is based on a legend that I read when younger. The
whistlers are ducks with haunting calls which foretell
serious events, e.g. an imminent death. This legend varies
from county to county but in this particular version, six
whistlers search for a seventh. When the last whistler is
found, the world ends. It is a haunting legend made even
more poignant by the shrill call of these whistling ducks.)

'Tall Bird'. Kiran Patel (17)

The Injury

Dad brought him home
Last night.
All frozen and stiff.
A robin,
His scarlet waistcoat
A sullied brown
Gently I laid him
In a rag-filled box.
Tended him with water and seed.
He didn't eat a morsel,
Drink a drop.
A heavy lid
Dropped on his dew-drop eye.
He slept.
But in the morning,
He was
Dead.

Fergus Miskelly (11)
St Mary's Primary School,
Killyleagh, Co. Down, N. Ireland

Spider

Eight legs like flexible pipe-cleaners
Balancing on its tightrope web.
Ever inch of the dazzling, circular web
Is heavily guarded by sensitive trigger wires.
Each insect which touches his deadly fortress
Will quickly be pounced on
Then paralysed and eaten.

Left-overs are carefully wrapped up
In silky soft web.
If sleepy he will go into his larder
And sleep under the preserved insects
Hanging upon the ceiling.

Paul McNamara (14)
Ellen Wilkinson High School, Manchester

Misty Spiders' Webs

The spiders' webs
are sticky
The spiders' webs
have thin strong silk
but when it is misty
the webs have
precious droplets.
The delicate webs
sparkle in the soft wind.

Shaun Wilson (6)
Clover Hill First School, Norwich

Worm

Elementary
Undeveloped
Annelida.
Limbless
Boneless
Mindless
Shameless.
Welded into segments
Weathering and waning
Expressing no wanderlust
Wryly uncomplaining.
Meandering
Listlessly
Furtively
Pensively
Impotent
Inanimate
Inferior.
Infiltrate
Earth's
Jungle
And
Wait.

Kathy Mills (15)
Rainey Endowed School,
Magherafelt, N. Ireland

The Earthworms

Underground, very
Darkly, noiselessly
Very patiently

With the strength of our bodies, we
Burrow through loam
Acquire the dark.

Nobody sees us
Though gardeners praise us
Unseen and unheard

We are irreplaceable
Our burrows essential
To all great and small.

Meek, and unthought of
Humble and ordinary
Mean and lowly

We diet on leaves
Unwanted debris
Tasteless nutrition.

We are long
We are slimy
We are bristled and segmented

We are monarchs of the underground
Heirs to the earth
Tomorrow we shall inherit the world.

Paula Jackson (13) Lymm, Cheshire

The Ladybird

Tiniest of tortoises
Your shining back
Is like an egg of red
With spots of black.

How lightly you walk
Across this land
Of valleys and crevasses,
That is my hand.

Your tiny black legs,
So small, so thin,
Their touch is like feather
Upon my skin.

There, spread out
Your wings and fly.
No frailer creature
Beneath the sky.

Leoma Rushton (9)
Ysgol y Clogau, Dolgellau, Gwynedd
(Highly commended)

Stupid Moth!

Stupid Moth!
Hitting yourself senseless against
A false light, of your greed
Your self-destruction.
When out in the cool night
There is food and love
And happiness.
But you must pursue
The brightness and so die!

Marina Kiely (13) Bath, Avon

'On Tuesday It Rained'. Nusrat Ahmad (5) (Highly commended)

Butterfly

As the priest drones on
In the pulpit in the church,
The little child sits upright
Trying not to fidget inside the harsh material

126

A flurry of colour catches her eye
Up high in the rafters
A rainbow trapped on wings
Flutters around the church
In the form of a tiny butterfly.

The child holds her breath
Transfixed, in awe, delighted,
Her eyes follow the colours
As the little creature skims
Through the air, high up in the vaulted roof
And down towards the priests,
Unseen by anyone but the child.

As the priest drones on
In the pulpit in the church
The little child watches the butterfly,
Which has taught her more
Than the vicar's meaningless and
Monotonous preaching.

Has taught her about
Life and Beauty, and Love and Happiness
The little wings gliding down towards her
As if to bid her goodbye
And then the butterfly
Blows out of the door,
A spectrum of colours on the wind.

Ruth Platt (13)
Rowley Bristow Hospital, Woking, Surrey

The Water Snake

A long, shiny body,
Slimey and Slithery,
Could
Just!
Be seen, among the long grass.
Its brown, rough camouflage hiding it
It slid twisting and turning near the water's edge.
It's fork tongue slithering in and out,
And sharp eyes
With a squint!
But!
Suddenly
A ripple in the water, could be heard.
Hiss!
Danger
It felt my presence.
And like a dart
Disappeared between the reeds,
Its shiny, slithery body slithered,
Silently away
And the snake was . . .
Gone!

Stefanie Ager (13) and Nicola Fergusson (13)
Darrickwood School, Orpington, Kent

The Crocodile Keeper

Amongst the misty, murky marsh,
The crocodile lies hard and harsh,
This greedy-minded log of wood,
He'd eat you all up if he could!
He lurks among his muddy dwelling,
And I'm afraid there is no telling
Which one of us he'd like to taste,
Which one of us he'd mince to paste.
And so, my dears, now just in case,
You'd better go in quite a haste.
Oh look! There comes his scaly face!
He's moving forward at fast pace!
His jaws a-chompin' up 'n' down!
His eyes a-rollin' roun' 'n' roun'
His teeth a-snapping', tail a-whackin'!
Mouth is waterin' lips a-smackin'!
But all you have to do and say
To calmly make him walk away
Is 'Sorry Croc, to bring you sorrow,
You'll have your *proper* meal tomorrow!'

Karen Heath (11)
St Martin's Middle School, Epsom, Surrey

Wild Wolf

Wild wailing wolf,
A strong back
Gleaming red eyes
A jagged coat
Proud bushy tail
Howling cry
Black wet nose
Moves steadily
Lives in a den
Eats rabbits
Fierce warning voice
Cruel beady eyes
Sharp teeth
Evil grin.

Jeanette Pearson (7)
Bolton, Lancs

The Spoils of Winter

Severed stems,
Brought down by the weight of the ice,
Seep thick white blood,
From blackened vessels.
A frog,
Trapped within a circular prison of reeds,
Didn't escape Winter's grasp;
He remained embedded in the ice,
Like a fly suspended in a lump of amber,
Until the thaw.
And then his translucent skin,
As frail as a bud's sepal,
Became swollen and wrinkled,
Like a hand that has been in water too long.

Lucas Marshall (14)
The Mountbatten School, Romsey, Hants
(Highly commended)

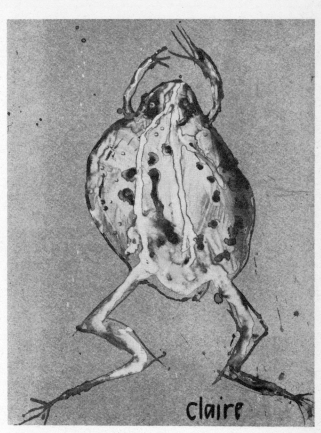

'Toad', Clare Savage (7)

Cats

Cats stalking
sleeping washing

Claws scratching
pulling tearing

Tails swashing
swishing waving

Eyes staring
glaring looking.

Shaun Nee (7)
Bulwell St Mary's School, Notts

Cat's Eyes

His eyes are like coal from the middle of hell,
Ever so still,
Something moves
Suddenly his eyes turn to the left,
Then to the right
Nothing there.
He swings his snaky tail,
His body brindled,
He bares his curved sharp claws.
Morning comes,
His eyes aren't so bright any more,
They just twinkle in the sunlight,
He lies on the rug,
Licking his silky fur.

Sherrie Swan (11)
Darrickwood School, Orpington, Kent

My Lovely Pussy Cat

We have a cat her name is Lizzy
Her games make me fairly dizzy.
She licks, she purrs, she sits and begs
And plays with my mum's pegs.
When she scratches at the door
You would think she's not been fed before.
She even rides upon my swing
And doesn't seem to fear a thing.
Now she's curled up fast asleep,
Is she really counting sheep?
No, she's not. She's counting mice,
My pussy cat's life is rather nice.

Joanne Mathieson (7)
William Alvey School, Sleaford, Lincs

Nightfall

The moon spreads its light across the sleeping villages
And the creatures of the night awaken to hunt their
prey.
The fox comes creeping through the forest
Searching for the rabbits and mice that run about in
the grass.
The scaring noises are coming to play with the
night-time sky.

Dheya Biswas (6)
Bedgrove County First School, Aylesbury, Bucks
(Highly commended)

'Boy and Rabbit'. Michelle Spratt (16)

I Love the Rabbit

I love the rabbit,
So furry and nice,
It is a pity it isn't a cat,
Because they catch mice.

Claire Parsons (7)
Heathfield J.M.I. School,
Darlington

134

Harbour

Freshwater cold,
Mackintoshed: silver-green corpses.
Stare outwards, land drowned,
Accusingly plead in one direction

Barred down,
Haul worn: boundaries of evil
Layered bizarrely: links of russet chain
No revolt against their closeness.

Dead meat,
Mouths hooked, hungrily wide.
Crevices – gulping gills suffocated.
Splash, drip onto warm, sunned stoned.

Shadowing onlookers,
The proud master; work still a novelty.
Not unique, but certainly a worthy catch,
Familiar linger of salt stench . . .

Stranded as mermaids,
free: yet forever captured – since
that one, dynamic leap.
A slight smile – one vision,
Yes,
The teasing trickle of another tide.

Maxine Harfield (14)
The Crestwood School, Eastleigh, Hants

The Mole

A small, but industrious spy burrows his way
Along the dark corridors of a large underground
   mystery.
This place, a world that only a small minority
Has ever experienced, is home for this
Informer and his many acquaintances.

The creature glides along a familiar area
Of tunnel, searching for signs of unwelcome visitors.
He will make sure that those who would dare
To intrude, shall suffer with such great severity,
That they would never return to this perilous stretch.

So small and gentle in its outer skin is this creature,
   that on assumption,
It would not cause such a sense of dominance.
It is only with its associates that this animal
Would indulge in such violent outbreaks.
After all, what power against mankind has one,
   individual mole?

Lynda Arrowsmith (14)
Acklam Grange School, Cleveland

The Chase

When they grazed I watched, when they drank I
   watched,
As they climbed the hill I waited, while they rested I
   was there,
I was waiting, I was watching, I was thinking . . .

We were all peaceful, all was so calm, all was so still,
Nothing seemed bad, nobody realized the evil was
   near.
And should we have noticed, when wind did not
   blow,
Where could we shelter, where was there to go?

They climbed, they drank, they were not at all
   fearing,
The sun shining so peacefully down on the earth.
But I knew, I was there, I knew the moment, I knew
   the time,
And it came like a flash of bright lightning. I took it,
   and ran!

What could we do, where could we run?
The river! The crystal glaze smashed as the herd
jumped.
Down into the water. Speed was now, the speed of
light.
We ran, he ran, but we were too fast.
So he was left staring, glaring . . . at us.

Emma Lloyd (11)
Arnett Hills School, Rickmansworth, Herts

The Clear Round

The starting bell sounded,
The clapping ceased,
The stride of the big bay horse increased.

He flicked his ears,
As he eyed the gate,
But he gathered himself a fraction too late.

He caught it on front,
The whole jump swayed,
The crowd they gasped, somehow it stayed.

They were cantering on,
The next jump was tall,
But this one was no trouble at all.

Four jumps after this,
He cleared them all,
The last fence loomed, it was a red and white wall.

She felt the power
As he left the ground
He flew over the top,
Applause rang round
And then the green Tannoy boomed
   CLEAR ROUND!

Paula Raven (11) and Caroline Knowles (12)
Simpson County Combined School, Milton Keynes

Frightened

Standing in a barn
among dung and straw
Is the young Charolais calf.
His liquid eyes full of fear,
His muscles tensed, ready to bolt,
He backs slowly away
Back to the comfort of his
mother's presence
And the taste of his mother's
warm milk.
His eyes, no longer filled with
fear but with comfort and
contentment,
The young Charolais calf.

Jim Sykes (11)
County J. and I. School,
Bradford-on-Avon, Wilts

The Hunter

Am awa oot wi' the gun the nicht
Tae see if I've caught a fox
Bit as I crooch doon the back o' the dyke I see a craw.
I fix the gun tae my shooder an aim wi' a ma skill.
An' bang, doon comes the craw, toplin' and tumblin'
    thru the pine branches.
That wis the end o' a peer crator's life.
Bit' at cartridge saved a fair bit o' barley.

James Middleton (10) Kinellar School, Aberdeenshire

139

A Winter Picture

It's a glistening winter's evening
and why do you hear a trotting sound?
It's the white winter horse.
She trots along the white hill,
she likes the winter's cold.
She does not need a home you know.

White fluffy snow flakes drifting by and by
Little bits of grass peeping through the snow,
the grass is small and tender.
The horse's main and tail streaming in the moonlight
Her eyes shine in the starlight.

Isabelle Weil (7) Torpoint Infants School, Cornwall

The Magical Unicorn

I am the Magical Unicorn
I don't eat stars,
I eat cheese from the moon.
I drink silver juice from the brightest planet.
I am the Magical Unicorn
I don't wear fur,
I wear white skin with angels' wings plunging out of it.
I don't live on the moon,
I live in the Milky Way.
I am the Magical Unicorn
I don't like the plough it spoils the atmosphere,
I like picking moon flowers.
I don't fear devils
I fear star ghosts.

Theresa Balcombe (10) Rye, E. Sussex

The Polar Bear

The polar bear's
    fur is
  like sugar.
   His nose
    is like a
black plum.

Jason Fields (9)
New Milton Junior School, Hants

'St Mark's'. Stephen Penders (17)

Enigma

Wearing dizzy circles round and
Round the murky, sloshy globe of
Moulding water, the deadly Poadlet
Lurks. Relentlessly, it hacks at the
Lush olive undergrowth growing wild in
This danger-patch. Many small beasts will
Meet their end within the jaws of this
Fierce amphibious tyrant. Its small
Black head twitches in all directions,
Seeking its innocent prey. The
Jet-coloured snake-like object attached
To the head jerks constantly to and fro,
Rippling the once calm depths. Then
A 'something' prompts the entire mini-universe
To tilt. Again the empire shakes,
Tilting the other way. There is a scurry as
Thousands of microscopic mechanisms struggle
To the sanctuary of the plant life. As for the
Elopdat, he merely rolls over and
Over, until now, the worst comes. The whole
Of the globe has rolled over, and appears to
Be shrinking . . . shrinking . . .
The Tapdole gazes upwards, where its stare is
Returned by twin emerald marbles, which
Glare down at this tiny, struggling life-form,
Fighting for life as it lies on the thick grey
Carpet, its life support seeping away into its
Own private Underworld under the floorboards.
The marbles move as one body towards the evil
Toadpet, enthralled by its slinky black skin,
    shimmering

In the light. In a flash, a sharp talon pierces
The surface of the Poletad's protective flesh,
Killing it instantly. The paw drops the dead
Tadpole, which is immediately devoured by the
Large, black tom-cat.

Kate Haworth (11) Poulton-Le-Fylde, Lancs

'The Circus Act'. Katherine Holmes (11)

The Performing Monkey

An old withered face,
A young withered face
As the old man turns his crank
The monkey dances,
And gaily leaps,
Wearing its merry clothes,
An array of red,
A gush of gold,
And the pitter patter of light feet,
The sunken eyes,
The crooked hands,
The old man in his glamour of rags,
A stun of dullness,
A creak of a crank,
And a little dancing monkey.

Moray Teague (13)
Barnard Castle School, Co. Durham

Wild Horses

The wild horses jump and toss,
In the misty air,
The hot sun beats hard,
On the sandy ground,
White man rounds the horse,
It breaks its herding cage,
The white horse starts a tantrum,
In a fierce rage.

The animal starts to cavort,
The men throw a rope round his neck,
Soon they are dragged along,
The horse may have a chance to flee
Away from white man's town,
Now he is free and wild,
As wild,
As wild,
Can be.

Daniel Abbott (9) Warrington, Cheshire

'Halt at the Jump'. Rosanne Edwards (10)

The Natural World

Acrostic Poem

The sno**W**
is l**I**ke a dust-
cover waiti**N**g to be
lif**T**ed by
th**E** spring
deco**R**ators.

John Ford (13)
Abingdon High School, Wigston Magna, Leics

First Signs of Spring

The sun shines higher in the sky
A hanging ball of gold.
The red bulb of the peony
Pushes through the dead
Of the winter past.
Tulip bulbs like stalagmites
Push through the soil.
The bud-filled twigs
Of cherry, aspen, oak.
Old deserted house martin nests
In the gables of the school.

The hope of new life fills
The songs of the birds.
The yellow flowers of Jasmine
Here to greet the grass.
The multitude of greenery
Ready for the Spring.
Birds glide through the sky
To the song
Of promised joy.
The young nettles grow
At the feet of the elders.

Henry Smith (11)
The Beacon School,
Amersham, Bucks

Snowdrops

Snowdrops
are a sign
that winter's past,
their whiteness
lightens up dark places.
They shine in the black,
like stars in the sky.
There they stand
like white bells,
in white dresses
and green caps,
white as the snow
in a dark world.

Kristy Derbyshire (7)
St John's C.E.
Primary School,
Dukinfield, Cheshire
(Highly commended)

'Snowdrops'. *Scott Hayes (9)*

Storm

We knew it was coming,
When the clouds merged and gathered together –
An influx of black sheep
And hung low in the sky, pulsing with foreboding.

Suspended and silent
Sending heat into their created dark,
So that air became close
And we all cringed at their hot doom-like prophecy.

And, as the clock struck twelve,
Still no one departed from the room; but
Stayed waiting together,
To watch the fight between the demons of the sky.

The first resplendent flash
Of battle illuminated the sky
Momentarily, to reveal
With vivid brightness, the intensity of the wound

Which it had created.
Then came the rumble of conflict, which launched
Bolts of incandescent
Splendour across the luminous arc of the heavens.

Then, abruptly the conflict
Ceased. The air buzzed in expectation, but
After the night cooled, and
The silence was gone, we knew the outcome:
For the wind wailed,
And the clouds wept,
At the loss of their masters.

Allison Roberts (14)
Acklan Grange School, Middlesbrough, Cleveland

The Storm That Night

Then the flat water rippled, slapped into billows,
And came tumbling and chasing amongst the crests
   and the hollows.
Waves curled, spun into foam as they fought and
   followed;
Then black sudden dark. The storm-giants heaved
   and wallowed –
Roaring, they trod water and joyously bellowed.

But next day, fishing in smooth water for flickering
   minnows,
We splashed shoreward in sand and caressing
   shallows.

Arnold Hunt (15) Hendon, London
(Highly commended)

The Hunt

An ominous rumbling echoes round the sky,
Bouncing from cloud to cloud.
The Sun, sensing danger
Dons an overcoat of cloud,
Concealing itself.
As a shy child, hidden in its mother's skirts,
Or a hunted animal in undergrowth
Its tormentors arrive
Rain, Wind and Thunder.
Crashing round the sky.
Calling,
Teasing,
Beckoning.
Thunder seizes a spear of light, and,
With a roar like a thousand hungry lions,
Hurls it through the misty barrier.
The wind rushes to retrieve it
Dodging between clouds
With the swiftness and agility
Of a cheetah.
The rain rides on its back
Scattering handfuls of his glistening confetti
Over all below

Sun will not betray itself,
Tormentors grow angrier
Thunder roars, Wind screams
Rain dispersed its hardest weapon
Hail.
All three, calling
Daring Sun to show itself
Sun cowers lower
Within its warm protective boundary
Thunder rages up and down the sky
Tearing open muslin clouds
With a rod of burning iron.
Wind follows
Rain resplendent on her back
At last
They disconsolately shuffle away
Defeated.
The Sun peeps out
Chuckling
Victorious.

Kerry Elkins (13)
Lynn Grove High School,
Gorleston, Norfolk

Autumn Wind

The Autumn wind is cold, I have this lovely feeling.
The leaves twist and twirl and the apples sway and
   fall.
I see a squirrel scampering down a tree with a
   hazelnut in his mouth;
The leaves are russet brown and golden orange;
The berries are dancing for joy and the conkers are all
   holding hands.
Woosh, woosh it's a whirly wind, I sing and I dance.
In the Autumn wind the wind is running through my
   hair;
The whirly wind is tearing down the trees.
Cold leaves are crispy yellow, at sundown the wind
   comes again –
Nuts fall down like skipping ropes.
A nut fell down on my head brrrrrrrrrr I'm cold.

Zoe Fowler (7)
Oaklands County Infants School, Chelmsford, Essex

The Angry Sea

The sea goes bash, bash, bash
Against the seaweedy rocks.
With a spray of twenty feet high
Waves towering above the rocks
Like snow witches taking snow
And throwing it.
Rocks like dinosaurs
Tall tyrannosaurus and long brontosaurus.
The waves against the rocks

Are dark, dark, dark as a cave.
Seaweed sticking against the rocks
Looks like hair on your head.
The sea crashes and smashes
Bits off the rocks
Like cutting down a tree.
Spray as white as
Snow, snow, snow
A snow blizzard.
Roaring, clashing waves
A lion roaring, roaring, roaring,
Shouting, howling, rumbling
Like a big hungry wolf
Grumbling winds blowing the sea
Making big, big whirlpools.

Paul Metherell (7)
The Butts School, Alton, Hants

Bubbles

Rotating spheres,
Hovering in the air
Reflections,
Curved into the shape of the bubble.
Drifting, floating,
Bouncing off soft surfaces,
Whirling up into the air
A swirling cascade of colour
Then the bubble bursts,
Leaving nothing,
Where before there was a perfect wonder.

Alison Balmond (10)
Peover Nether C.E. Primary School, Cheshire

The River

I gurgle
Twisting and turning
I go
Babbling,
Tinkling,
Dripping over rocks
For I am a little river.
Now I am bigger
Fish swim in me
High above I see
Wellington boots.
Man builds houses beside me
I am powerful
Suspension bridges hang above me
But I am spoiled
Muddy am I
There I end in the sea
But I do not die
For high above
I am still young.

Susanna Tayler (6)
Ecclesall Infant School, Sheffield

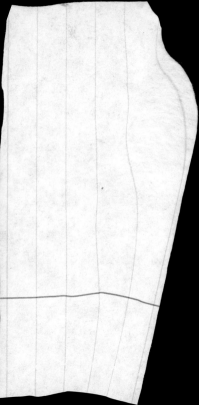

RL⟶ER

cream

The Autumn Bride

Our world has turned to jewels in a crown.
Worn by a bride.
The cobwebs are her dress of lace hung with pearls
 of dew.
The misty grey of bonfire smoke makes a veil around
 her face.
Her golden wedding ring made from polished corn
Rests on her cold white finger.
She carries the colours of autumn,
Red, black, orange, yellow, brown.
Sprinkled with diamonds of frost.

Frances Maclennan (8)
Avenue Middle School, Norwich

Water

A waterfall crashing down
    Lashing against the rocks,
Roaring down a mountain side
    And bashing the water at the bottom.
Ear-piercing, amazing waterfall,
    Like a person sliding down the stairs,
The rumbling sound is so loud.

A puddle in the road
    So still I can see my face in it.
        A drop of oil in the puddle makes a rainbow.
    My boot splashes down and out comes the water.

Mark Angus (7)
Hampreston C.E. First School, Wimborne, Dorset

Bonfire Night

The colours are beautiful,
Galloping gold, silver fray of
Fizzing fountain
Dazzling green comes from
traffic lights.

As the flames licked up
Into the air,
I heard a screaming rocket
And a screaming Catherine Wheel.

The sour silver savagey bonfire
Roaring ruby flames
Licking up into the air
Golden-yellow and ruby red.

I smelt some hot dogs
And a piece of cake
Next day it was wet
And miserable.

Nathaniel Seviour (7)
St Peter's C.E. Primary School,
Market Bosworth, Warks

The Night Horseman

The Firebirds pulling the Sun chariot
Fly behind the hills for
The horseman of the night is coming
On his horse,
His coal-black horse with silver spots
Upon his black hide,
And his dark helmet
With the silver crest
And his cloak of darkness
Spreading out behind him,
Enveloping the world in its folds
As he gallops off.

Jeremy Beacock (11)
West Jesmond Junior School,
Newcastle-upon-Tyne

Snow Is Falling Gently

Snow is falling gently
It's like a smashed cloud that's exploded
into millions of pieces.
I wonder who would have done this thing?
I do not know.

Andrew Thomas (7)
Hampden Park Infant School,
Eastbourne, E. Sussex

'Winter Landscape', Lucie Akerman (12)

Winter

In winter when it snows,
I go tobogganing and get cold toes,
I step in the ice which is crunchy and nice
and when I get home my nose glows.

Victoria Woodhead (6)
Millfield School, Street, Somerset

Winter

White,
Smooth blanket.
Silently fallen,
Silently there.
Covering the surface
Of all around.
Most of all,
Covering,
Silent ground.

The tree.
Black, stark,
Silhouetted.
Deprived of glory,
Bare tree.
Snow covered,
Overladen,
White on black.

The fence.
Rows of wooden poles
With bars across.
Blackened with age,
Submerged with snow,
Light on dark.

White on black.
Light on dark.
Silent ground.

Hannah Steventon (12)
Woodbridge, Suffolk

False White

I sit and stare at the whiteness,
At crystalline flakes of purity,
Which tumble and spiral
From a candy-floss sky,
To blanket the earth, to cleanse,
But belie.

Eric Houston (15)
Rainey Endowed School,
Magherafelt, N. Ireland

My Snowman

I built a snowman very tall,
I hoped and hoped it would not fall.
I put a hat upon his head,
'Now you're finished,' I proudly said.
'You look so well with your carrot nose,
I'll have to find you some warm clothes.'
I put a scarf around his neck
I tied it very tight.
'See you in the morning,'
I said to him.
But he melted during the night.

Samantha Hill (7)
Millington Primary School, Portadown

Snow

The first flakes fell
Slowly, silently against
The window pane;
Stealthily, drowsily
Drifting down,
Flake upon flake.
Then a sudden creaking
Of doors and windows
Gave indication of
The blizzard to come,
Twisting, twirling incessantly,
A manic dance
Obscuring the view.

Bayard Molan (12)
Debenham High School,
Woodbridge, Suffolk

Acrostic

Sting in the tail, they say, looms in the air above you;
Clasp your talons, bloated round prey.
Order to death, courage torn in two.
Run now from the ripped scrap, hawkshadow scours
    ground,
Pray for your vengeance, your knowledge is
    profound.
Intelligence served you little, when it did it served
    well.
Orion thus lies poisoned, in stars and in hell.
Now go from the shadow! Rise in might! Ring the
    knell!

Luke Merales (14)
Lynn Grove High School, Gt Yarmouth, Norfolk

(Orion the Great Hunter was finally brought to justice by
Scorpio the Scorpion. Both died and became star con-
stellations in the sky.)

In Time of War

In the Trenches

The biting wind and bitter cold,
A gnawing hunger
And a longing to be back home.
Mud and snow
And a nagging fear,
Will I live to see next Christmas?
Or will this become my grave?
I long to see my family,
To know that they are safe.
But Christmas this year is in a muddy trench,
Rain, sleet and snow,
Low temperatures and freezing cold.
Do the people at home think about me?
This trench has become my home,
Maybe it will be my last.

Emma King (11)
Roberttown C.E. J. and I. School, W. Yorks

Over the Top

As I wait for the signal I smell fear
  I know I cannot stay behind,
For if I do I will be shot. It happens you know
  If you refuse you are shot, there and then.

The others are getting ready,
  They're going over too, with me
I see the barbed wire, that we must cross
  The place where most of us will be shot.

Terrified, that I am, but proud, I am
  Risking my life, for my country
I check that I have everything I need,
  Ammo, helmet and . . . and a family photo.

I hear gun shots then . . . nothing
  It cannot be long now
Suddenly I hear it, loud and shrill
  I hear gun shots then . . . screams.

The guns roar like lions,
  I play dead man
Eventually there is silence again
  Perhaps they think everyone is dead.

Kenneth Irving (11)
Struthers Primary School, Troon

The Young Soldier

The body lies caught fast in the steel spider's web
Twisted in grotesque shapes
His arm thrown over the steel
The hand hangs limply
The other hand grips the web
And a steel spine impales it
His legs lie in a bath of blood
The trousers ripped and torn
The rifle he carried is half buried in mud
His eyes which once sparkled with life are grey and
    dull
They stare blankly at the sky
His face caked in mud is ash grey
It is twisted in agony frozen forever in death

Matthew Hayes (14)
St Anthony's RC School, Middlesbrough, Cleveland

Green Meadows

Green meadows swaying in the sun,
The war is over, it's all gone and done,
Red, red poppies lay in sheaves
Upon those who died at the mercy of their beliefs.
Golden sun, oh, golden sun,
You look upon what we have done.

Rowena Martin (11)
Simpson County Combined School, Milton Keynes

Requiem

The day dies quietly
On a whispered breath, blown faintly
Over barren heath.
Twilight dulls the pulsing red
To a grey-black ooze
Like mud.

Evening wraps its shroud about the place,
And the moon on rising
Heaves a bitter sigh,
Her mournful eye encompassing the fruits
Of rage.

Silent, the grave of evening,
Following the death throes of the day.
And strewn about,
The shells of men
Lie rotting.

Pamela McKay (16)
Ellen Wilkinson High School, Manchester

Peace of Mind

I

You who have not seen death,
Say you would kill with ease
To keep your long-won freedom.
But war veterans hesitate to
Tumble a man again into the
Heavy slop of a mud grave.
And so would rather cry
In peace behind white walls.
Today I have heard a soldier's
Latest scream, when he had thought
Himself blown up to heaven,
Fell to earth once more and
Stumbled on feet no longer his.

II

I have known a little girl
So charred and frozen, like
The day the lava spilled
Over all Pompeii and kept
Its people nameless; her mother
Only knew her for her size
And height. Yet as the small
Coffin wended in at the
Front door, the mother rushed
Out through the back and
Silent tears fell on the lawn.

III

I daresay you know the other
Anguish too. The black figure
Backtracks across the Diamond,
Later, out of den, the plastic
Smears his features. The gunman's
Wife who gave herself a chill reception
In the stream; the next dawn found
Her face down, her nightdress was
Flecked with ravening foam.

IV

I daresay you might still kill,
Forgetting the bin-lid rattle of
Machine-guns that haunts our dreams.
And nightmare flickers like the
Flames past our windows, whispering
We are never free until the
Earth has rolled us round and
Let us sleep secure.

Rosemary Cowan (17)
Co. Londonderry, N. Ireland
(Award winner)

The Wilderness

A monstrous red sun
Glaring from a harsh sky
Illuminates the landscape
With an intense white light
Over crumbling, shattered buildings,
Splintered and scattered,
And trees blackened, mutilated.
Cruel cracks split
The once fertile land,
Stretching into an interminable horizon.
Shadowless,
Noiseless,
The silence suffocates
All.

An avalanche of bricks,
And a hand appears,
An arm, a body . . .
Finally a face:
One eye staring
From a confusion
Of melted flesh, skin and bone.
Disbelief shudders uncontrollably
Through the naked body,
Like a puppet's,
Needing a sign.

The fiery ball in the sky
Forms sweat
On decomposing skin.
A slight wind begins to blow

Eeringly.
The body –
Perhaps a man –
Stumbles onwards,
Studying the surroundings,
Rummaging in rubble;
Searching for a sign.

The sun journeys onwards,
Ever nearing the blackened earth.
As he plods on,
The man's eye
No longer wanders aimlessly.
Now despair is rising
There is a stabbing in his stomach,
A rasping in his throat,
His tongue flicks out of its hole,
Moistening the edges
Of the cavernous opening.
A heap of debris
Forms a sudden hope,
Triggering an unconcious memory
In a far from logical mind.

And the man runs,
Steps beating, soft and rhythmical,
Breath gasping, quick, shallow.
He reaches the pile,
Starts to scrabble
Among rocks,
Bricks and wood
With his bare hands,
Animated at last,

Desperate for a sign.
At last he collapses
Blood oozing
From cuts
On arms and legs,
His hands
Still clasping
An unmovable rock.

No direct light shines now,
But only an iridescence,
Glowing through the clouds,
Which chase ferociously
Across a shifting, purple sky,
That seems to threaten
As it descends
Towards the earth.
The wind howls through
The infirm shells of humanity,
On the unmoving plain.
The cruel cold wakes the man,
Whose weak, white body
Is frozen as if in a negative
On the bleak, blackened surroundings.
He turns,
His single eye
Darting about,
Wishing
For someone,
Something,
A sign of life.
'NO!'
His piercing scream is
Instantaneously drowned

By the wind's
Eternal crying, howling
Across the wilderness:
A former civilization,
Destroyed by a nuclear bomb.

Lara Burns (17) Cambridge

'*Farmer and His Wife*', *Paul Lee (14)*

Paper Poppies

Every year we celebrate the war,
Heads of State lay wreaths,
With smug sadness,
A formality.
Families remember and tell their grandchildren,
With tears of pride,
'How brave he was.'
Wartime stories,
Sirens and shelters,
Softened, maybe, by today's life,
Blurred by the indisputable assurance that,
We won.

But are there winners?
In a game with life?
Thousands 'lost',
Families dying,
But,
We won.

What about the 'losers'?
They don't celebrate the killing of their men,
Young men,
Young, strong, brave men.
Fighting for the shimmering mirage of,
Their Country.
'How sad,' you say, 'but –
We won.'

Remember, too, the innocent bystanders,
Caught up in the web of war,
The spider of Death,

Lashed out,
Broke the thin, silver thread of life.
If they survived,
They had to continue,
Knowing their friends, families and thousands of
    others,
Suffered bloody deaths,
Buried alive by falling rubble,
Burned alive by the bomb's glare,
A noiseless killer,
A ruined city,
Modern-day Pompeii,
Once a living, working community.
Then a flash,
Devastation from above,
A dead city.
Dead.
Dying.
Bleeding.
Crying
Crying for life.
And we say there are winners.

There is no glory in war.
In killing,
Maiming.

So lay your paper poppies,
Red for blood,
Not Victory.
And when you bow your head,
Your mind blank,
Think of the 'losers',
We did not win.
Death won.

Jacey Lamerton (13) Margate, Kent

175

Borderlines

He saw them right enough.
His mind went Border Patrol
As he searched for his licence.
But in his heart thumped
A peculiar pain as they
Swarmed around the headlamps.
He didn't make a move, not yet,
He wasn't sure if he'd heard
Alright and anyway the cold
Steady drizzle put him off
On a night when he should
Be by a good turf fire.
And so they opened the cab
Door to wrench him out
In one firm, cloying grasp.
He looked and thought to
See a hardened Catholic face
With black beret and sleeked eye
But saw instead a blond man,
Disinterested and with a green
Muffler. One shot blasted
Him into the sodden ditch.
They found him later and
His cattle truck; they cleaned
Him up so people admired his
Neat grey coffin suit but
Avoided looking at the
Mess where his face had been.

Rosemary Cowan (17)
Co. Londonderry, N. Ireland
(Award winner)

It Makes You Think

Life Is

Life is love, love it
Life is food, eat it
Life is hate, despise it
Life is God, worship it.

Life is work, take it
Life is fun, laugh it
Life is sad, cry it
Life is happy, enjoy it.

Life is hurt, feel it
Life is lazy, sleep it
Life is death, survive it
Life is life, live it.

Michael Aspinall (14)
Pudsey Grangefield
School, Leeds

Death

Death approached me
Spindly.
It called out in soft, wheedling tones.
But I did not want it.

Death grabbed me
Roughly.
I was unprepared for this surprise.
I had no power to fight.

Death has won me
Basically.
I am no longer my own person.
He has my soul.

Death can not keep me
Totally.
I can approach you in spirit
And you will cry for me.

Julia Marsden (16)
Guiseley, Leeds

Transplant

In death we find life,
In sorrow joy.
The ending of a song and beginning of another,
New life arising from the ashes of old life,
A dark cold winter means a fresh green spring –
Sadness brings new hope,
Thus sorrow and joy meet and become one.

Arwen Claydon (11)
Kilbowie Primary School, Clydebank, Glasgow

(*Teacher's Note:* This work was inspired by a television report of a successful organ transplant.)

Skull

Bloated, my great grey mass
Is crazed with cracks; age
Has polished me like smooth glass.

In the brain, ideas hum into flight,
Through a hive of swarming laughter
To layered honeycombs of thought.
But no mind flaps up from the skull;
Merely the motions of a well-built cage
Responding blindly to the brain's pull.

Yet, hollow globe of bone,
I grin wordlessly long ages after
My fragile tenants are gone.

Arnold Hunt (15) Hendon, London
(Highly commended)

Earth Report

There are halls with many flashing lights,
People gather there late at night,

And when they come out it is morning,
Their pockets are empty.

Great animals roam about,
Swallowing and spewing out people,

Who consider it quite an honour,
And line up to be chosen along their route.

The young of the species
Gather in great sprawling buildings

And receive punishment from elders.
They stay there for twelve years,

And when they come out for the last time
Their eyes do not sparkle as before.

Timothy Watson (13)
The King's School, Canterbury, Kent

The Robot's First Birthday Party

Happy birth
Birthday hap-
Py - - - - birth
Jolly present
Presents given
Given jolly
Present happy
Birthday gâteau
Fruit 'n nutcake
With some presents

Given to-you
Happy birthday
Jolly happy
Presents plenty
Plents presenty
Food for all-ie
Jolly goody!

END

Louise Singleton (14)
Ilkley, W. Yorks

Child and Art

Eager, wandering, quivering hands,
Creating, producing, building in sand,
And clay and paint and wool and brick;
Cutting and carving, making things stick.

A need to squeeze, to touch and mould;
A genius here, to have and hold.

Child and Art,
A beginning, a need;
Talent which blooms
To flower from seed.

Jennifer Newell (16)
Sudbury, Derbyshire

'Tim is Reading a Comic', Katie Heath (8) (Highly commended)

Happiness

Happiness is a fleeting glimpse,
A moonbeam or a precious pearl,
We lose it unexpectedly,
As if it had slipped quietly,
Out of a carelessly opened door.
Marred by sorrow, pain or misery
It leaves us like a breath of wind

Hearts lie open to poison darts
Of sorrow, jealousy or anger,
Once it is regained
It is as if we had never lost it
Taking happiness for granted
As we do,
It surprises us when it returns,
Lifting a veil of oppression
And granting us lightness of heart
And light, carefree step
We know that we are happy again
It is enough.

Maria Goater (15) Bolton, Lancs

Another Postcard Home to Mars

Notes are little bits of paper
With patterns on them.

People hide them, and must be given
A present before they will give them away.

Politicians are humans who work for the People,
But ignore a person.

Voltaire happens when the sky malfunctions.
It sparks and bangs, and people are afraid

That it will break down and collapse,
Crushing them with its weight.

Christopher Tothill (14)
The King's School, Canterbury, Kent

'Self Portrait', Julie Lamb (16)
(Highly commended)

Upon Looking at a Monet

Helpless
Desire
So evocative
Caressing
Seduction in a classroom
By a long dead painter.
Why does it hurt
To look at
So much beauty?

Kate Kirby (17)
Pitlochry, Scotland

Either Sadness or Euphoria

They say that these are not the best of times,
But they're the only times I've ever known
And I believe there is a time for meditation,
In cathedrals of our own.

Now I've seen that sad surrender in my lover's eyes
And I can only stand apart and sympathise.
For we are always what our situations hand us,
It's either sadness or euphoria.

So we'll argue and we'll compromise,
And realize that nothing's ever changed.
For all our mutual experience,
Our separate conclusions are the same.

Now we are forced to recognize our inhumanity,
And reason coexists with our insanity.
So we choose between reality and madness,
It's either sadness or euphoria.

How thoughtlessly we dissipate our energies,
Perhaps we don't fulfil each other's fantasies
And as we stand upon the ledges of our lives
With our respective similarities,
It's either sadness or euphoria.

David Mathew (13)
Mill Vale Middle School, Dunstable, Beds

When I Open My Umbrella

When I open my umbrella of colours,
A thousand lights dazzle my eyes.
When I open my umbrella of wishes,
I wish for special presents.
When I open my umbrella of fear,
My knees shiver and shake.
When I open my umbrella of happiness,
All flowers fall on my head.
When I open my umbrella of goodness,
I dance about.

Tracy Stevens (7)
Tunbury C.P. School, Walderslade, Kent
(Highly commended)

'The Striker'. Patrick Loan (16)

Maybe Outside

Go and open the door.
Maybe outside there's a dish
And on that dish is a silver fish
With waving fins in a golden light.

Go and open the door.
Maybe outside there's a princess
Wearing a beautiful dress
Singing a song about herself.

Go and open the door.
Maybe outside there's a magic toy box
With a dancing doll and talking sailors,
And an elephant which plays with you all the time.

Go and open the door.
Maybe outside there's a swimming pool
With lots of laughing children in it.
Diving and swimming and playing.
Perhaps they'll let you join the fun.

Cathy Vincent (8)
Sandy Hill School,
St Austell, Cornwall

It . . .

Command from Brain:
Right Implement, out
Left Implement, wave on
Traffic from behind.

Command from Brain:
Execute previous action,
Left Implement, out
Right Implement direct traffic in front.

Command from Brain:
Right Implement continue
Left Implement direct traffic from behind.

Sound relayed to Brain:
Horn noise from vehicles
Visual optics locate object
Bus . . .
5 seconds to impact,
4, 3, 2, 1,
Message from Brain
Malfunction. MALFUNCTION.

Adrian Riley (14)
Pudsey Grangefield School, Leeds

Division

Mankind suffers unendingly
Maturing ages do not matter
But are matter themselves
Mother figure is
Technological development
Deviating from accepted lines
Population appears needed,
But used and abused,
Money is the affecting factor
Economists prefer resources
Politicians prefer sums and amounts
MONEY – makes the world go round –
ANTICLOCKWISE
KILLS
CORRUPTS
CONTROLS
. . . .

Timothy Locker (15) Ilkley, W. Yorks

Shadowplay
(A requiem for lost opportunities)

We stand behind a blank screen
Casting silhouettes that fall bleakly
Across our silent lives.
We move in unison, yet worlds apart,
Momentoes of long forgotten dreams
Form dusky images before our faces.
We never crossed the screen into the painted world
    beyond,
We waited for brighter days, new horizons –
But we waited until it was too late.
Now in darkness we move against the light
And hold our dark secrets to be forever untold,
And all that is left of our insignicant lives
Are the shadows in the long forgotten room.

Anna Gavela (14) Bolton School, Lancs

Sleep

Sleep, a slice of death,
Darkness in the mind,
Blackness through time,
Emptiness at night.

Sleep, shorter than death,
Longer than time.
Everlasting dreams,
Vivid as the sky.

Sleep, rest at last,
Joy every minute of the way,
Happiness for hours and hours,
Like living in a new world.

Christian Cerri (11)
St Edmund's School,
Hindhead, Surrey

Exploring

Sleep
    Sheltered by the wisdom of your infancy.
        Dreaming . . . exploring
           Creating brilliance from colour, splendour
             from sound.
If your reflections span all infinity . . .
    Then let the air that you breathe be silk, and sugar,
        and fine warm cloud.
        Let all the thwarted expectations of wakeful
          hours vanish.
Set out in quest of lemon-rind dragons, and
    ice-flowered angels and seas of torn and
    rain-barred sunlight.
Where silver song-birds, whose Icarus-wings near the
    sky, set the heavens swirling with violet fever.

For you are immortal . . . you are invulnerable
    You will exist into infinity.
If your reflections span all eternity . . .
    Then let the kaleidoscope sky revolve
        Let the entanglement of inexistence alter.
It will reveal muddling, murmuring, baring,
    kow-towing faces.
Explore . . . reach into the harmony
    Or soon . . . too soon, it will be too late.

Rachel Hughes (17) Alton Convent, Hants

Words

Words can be confusing to the ear,
Their versatility from love to hate,
From envy to friendship and greed to contentment.
Words inflict wounds no medic can fix.
They sometimes create relationships between two
strangers.
Words can make you annoyed and they baffle you.
They make a ray of light between their users, and
when there is silence the light fades.
Once said they are irreversible unless you are writing.
They stay in your mind and it is impossible to erase
them.
They hang on you if you didn't mean them,
And force you to apologize for using them.

Wayne Greenough (10)
Wellfield Wood School, Stevenage, Herts

Haiku

Haiku is not fun;
I really do not like it,
But I can write it.

Daniel Einon (13)
Fortismere School,
Tetherdown,
London

Ronald Reagan Haiku

Ron was an actor.
That's no excuse for thinking
All the world's his stage.

Simon Gee (14)
Abingdon High School,
Wigston Magna, Leics

'Pierrot', Davinder Matharall (13)

Inability to Write

Some days I awake with
The dull ache of a
Poem, trapped inside me, waiting
To unfurl; to spread its
Wings; to touch the
Sun.
I can feel it blooming, growing
Like a rosebud, caged within the
Depths of my heart, fragrance
Escaping through the bars,
Giving the world a taste of its
Beauty.
Poem; eager to live, to breathe, to sing.
Smooth, like a satin ribbon,
A brooklet of rippling words, sometimes
Too beautiful to confide to paper
With pen.

Helen Griffiths (13) Stockport, Cheshire

Time

Time swallows the future
And digests the past;
It is the trump card of Life.
Time decides on whose hour
Has slipped away
Like water through a thirsty man's fingers,
Or, who has time to come
Losing it in the waiting,

Time's one hand
Is long since bound,
While the other conducts
The Song of Precision;
It can mould the future
With its sensitive fingers
Or crush an Empire
With its clenched fists.

Run, run, try to beat the clock!
Run for ever –
Until Time itself says, 'Stop!'

Clare Hill (14) Baverstock School,
Birmingham

'A Voice Crying Alone
in the Wilderness'

I am God.
I caress the twisting trees with invisible fingers,
        Can you see me?
I wet the flowing rivers with a burning tongue,
        Can you hear me?
I tear open budding flowers with thorn-bloodied
  hands,
        Can you touch me?
Or, are you as blind as my Son's hunters?
I see you share your silver – but what am I to do?
Unleash my mighty wrath of anger?
Break the trees, drain the water?
Crumble the dead Earth
                into the void of my Kingdom . . .
No, vultures of my mind, I shall watch,
Like I have done for so long, oh, so long.
Frustrated
Exasperated
Old,
I tremble as you fumble through your wooden words.
But I shall wait, and weep a little, as you destroy
My Utopia
My dreams
My body.
      The wall is infinite between us –
        You must break free.
Only then will you see me.
Only then will you hear me.
Only then will you touch me.
I am God.
I am you.

Denise Wright (16)
Walsall, W. Midlands

Another Postcard Home to Mars

They poke coloured spheres with long, thin sticks,
On a green table, with holes in the sides.

They dress four-pronged objects,
Then bite them, and eat their clothing.

A big, red box stands on corners,
Begging for morsels of paper to eat.

It cannot digest them, this I know,
For a stomach-pump empties it twice a day.

The charitable stomach-pump then proceeds to
Give the food back to the people, to feed it again.

People are made in big, white buildings;
Three come out, where two went in.

John Pritchard (15) The King's School, Canterbury, Kent

Scarecrow

Crucified rags, marooned with senselessness,
a collected amnesia of plasma straw,
sack and jumble sale. Like an afterthought:
But is diligent, simple effective.

Clothed inhospitably, stink of Tramp,
its appearance comes with the weather:
Sponge soaked or dry like corrugated
Iron it keeps its gift; a voodoo of

turbulence to the plunderers of the
chocolate rich earth. The sentry of the
seed, partnered by the elements, gains lip
service from the beaver wind and leans on

the spine of days like a pit pony. As
clouds belly out and sieve I wonder on
the skull of Calvary, its strand of hair,
a pinnacle, still alive at the root.

Christopher Jones (15)
De Lisle School, Loughborough, Leics

The 1986 Cadbury's Poetry Competition

The Cadbury's Books of Children's Poetry contain about 200 selected entries from children of all ages and are illustrated with work from the National Exhibition of Children's Art.

If you would like to enter the 1986 competition whether in the Art, Craft or Poetry sections, you can write to this address for an entry form:

Cadbury's National Exhibition of Children's Art
Granby
Altrincham
Cheshire
WA14 5SZ
(Please enclose a stamped/addressed envelope)

Remember – you not only have a chance to feature in the *Cadbury's Fourth Book of Children's Poetry* but also to win a place on the Cadbury Italian Art Tour.

Index of titles

Index of authors

Also available from Beaver Books
The Cadbury's Second Book of Children's Poetry